Saint Vincent

Pray and Work
Motto of the Benedictines

Saint Vincent

A BENEDICTINE PLACE

Editor

Campion P. Gavaler, O.S.B.

Saint Vincent Archabbey

Latrobe, Pennsylvania   15650

1995

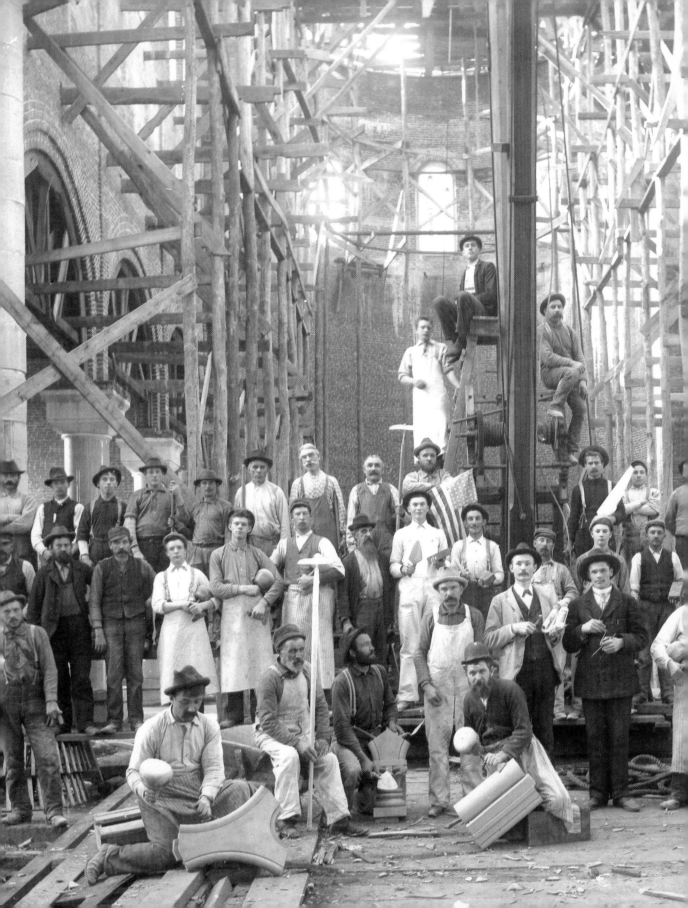

Contents

The Archabbot's Introduction

Saint Vincent: A Benedictine Place is a book of essays, poems, and illustrations whose purpose is to tell the story of Saint Vincent—Archabbey, College, Parish, and Seminary. As committees began planning our sesquicentennial events and projects, I observed that three aspects of Saint Vincent emerged in their discussions. Now as I reflect on the contents of the book while writing this introduction, I notice that the same three aspects are present: community, focus on the future, seeking God through prayer and work.

It is people who are Saint Vincent. The founding community of Benedictine monks has expanded to include many men and women who serve as partners with the Benedictines in a wide range of activities. In response to a request I recently made, hundreds of people who are part of our community in this broad sense submitted stories of their experience of Saint Vincent. I have read these responses, and am grateful for all of them. They will become a valued part of our sesquicentennial archives; many will be used in Saint Vincent publications. Although, by necessity, the number of contributors to this book is limited, the writers and photographers have captured something of the essential character of Saint Vincent, a Benedictine place.

Although we are grateful for our rich heritage of the past, our focus remains on the future, a future for which we share a common responsibility. Our Biblical, Catholic, and Benedictine tradition calls us to trust in the divine promise of a kingdom which is still to come. As Dr. Tranquilla in his essay puts it, our tradition is one of "outrageous hope."

Finally, our story represents a search for God in the everyday realities of life. A concern of Saint Benedict about a novice who wishes to join the community is that he "truly seeks God and...shows eagerness for the Work of God."

I trust that *Saint Vincent: A Benedictine Place* will be of interest to many people beyond those connected with Saint Vincent. The book is an expression of the desire of the entire Saint Vincent community to be in solidarity of hope with every family, parish, and community which is trying to live together in peace and is working to make our world a better place. Despite the powerful negative forces that seek to engulf us, we affirm life. We celebrate life.

Douglas R. Nowicki, O.S.B.

Acknowledgments

The production of *Saint Vincent: A Benedictine Place* was a community effort. The authors, first of all, deserve grateful acknowledgment for telling their stories about Saint Vincent. A person whose work does not directly appear in the book deserves special thanks. Most of the information about Boniface Wimmer and the early history of Saint Vincent is taken from *An American Abbot: Boniface Wimmer, O.S.B.*, published by the Archabbey Press in 1976. Jerome Oetgen wrote this biography while he was a member of the Saint Vincent monastic community.

Dennis Ciccone (White Oak Publishing, Ltd., Pittsburgh) was project manager. Michael Kolbrener (Kolbrener Associates, Pittsburgh) was the designer. Duane Rieder and Frank Walsh (Rieder and Walsh Photography, Pittsburgh) did the photography. Amilcare Pizzi (Milan, Italy) printed the book. Working with them was a pleasure.

Omer U. Kline, O.S.B., helped resolve many editing questions. David Kelly, O.S.B., coordinated preparation of manuscripts for the printer and helped with editing. Theresa Firment typed the manuscripts. I also want to acknowledge with gratitude a number of other people who helped in a variety of ways: John Benyo, Mary Brignano, Jean Boggs, S.C., Nathan M. Cochran, O.S.B., Wulfstan F. Clough, O.S.B., Vincent de Paul Crosby, O.S.B., Philip Hurley, O.S.B., Don Orlando, Chrysostom Schlimm, O.S.B., and members of the sesquicentennial committees (particularly the students).

Quotations from *RB 1980, The Rule of St. Benedict in English and Latin with Notes* and from "Article of the Reverend Boniface Wimmer, O.S.B., concerning the Missions of America in the Augsburg *Postzeitung*, 8 November 1845," reprinted as Appendix I in *Worship and Work* (3rd edition, 1994) by Colman Barry, O.S.B., are by permission of the Liturgical Press, Collegeville, Minnesota.

Campion P. Gavaler, O.S.B.

"Forward, always forward, everywhere forward. We cannot be held back by debts, by the difficulties of the times, by unfortunate years. Man's adversity is God's opportunity."

Boniface Wimmer, O.S.B.

Boniface Wimmer

Biblical, Catholic, Benedictine

Anniversaries have a way of nurturing nostalgia, but they are far more important as reminders of an original vision that can be a guide for the future. And when the monks of Saint Vincent reflect on the history and future of their institution, they must come to terms with the impressive figure of Boniface Wimmer. He did more than found Saint Vincent; he gave it a direction and a momentum that we still feel today. No one would deny his achievements as a founder and a missionary, but there are still misgivings by some about the direction that Wimmer gave to monasticism at Saint Vincent and indeed to the entire congregation of abbeys and priories that derives from his foundation. This would seem to be a good time to examine this crucial issue.

As we consider this question, we will notice how important it is to go beneath appearances to discover a spirit in Wimmer that belongs to the deepest level of religious experience. His faith was generally expressed in the traditional forms of his day, but at critical moments it was so creative and confident that it reminds us of great biblical believers like Abraham and David. His Catholic spirit was sometimes expressed in defensive and parochial ways, but his larger vision was as boundless and daring as that of his patron, Saint Boniface. Some questioned his understanding of monastic values, but his efforts were more fruitful than any other monastic renewal in modern times.

Vibrant Faith in Stagnant Times

The mid-nineteenth century was not a particularly glorious period in the history of the Catholic Church. The liturgy was rigid and ritualistic, preaching was florid and apologetical, and pious devotions seemed more important than biblically based spirituality. It is said that Wimmer was bored by the long and rambling speeches he heard at the First Vatican Council. In fact, the subject matter of that Council was not all that interesting. It is remembered for the definitions of papal infallibility and of the Immaculate Conception, but papal authority was already well established and the Immaculate Conception was already honored in the Church's liturgy. In fact, the Council was largely defensive in the face of rampant secularism. Wimmer was bored no doubt because he had little sympathy with defensive attitudes.

Attitudes are especially important where religion is at issue. There is a kind of faith that is concerned with right ideas and words but does not worry much about right attitudes. One can affirm orthodox creedal formulas and still live in a way that is so fearful and negative that

the meaning of the professed words is practically denied. It is strange indeed that one can affirm the resurrection of Jesus while living in a fearful and negative way and never be accused of heresy.

Boniface Wimmer may have lived in a theologically barren era but his faith was vibrant and positive and wonderfully fruitful. He manifested that confidence in God's presence in human history that is the characteristic of all the great believers. Like Abraham, the father of all believers (Rom 4:16), he trusted God's promises and dared to take risks when many counseled caution or retreat. "Forward, always forward, everywhere forward," he wrote. Like Israel's King David, Wimmer was attuned to the divine goodness that is revealed in history, promised in the future and, most of all, sensed in himself. Because of this inner confidence, he was remarkably unselfconscious. There was no hint in him of preoccupation with image. He would not even pose for a formal photograph, and he was embarrassed by well-deserved praise. His trust in God's goodness enabled him to focus all his attention on his work for others.

Wimmer also had some of the faults of David. He was so sure of himself and of the rightness of his mission that he sometimes did not take time to listen to others, to persuade them or to explain his intentions to them. Scholars like to point out that most of King David's sins came from his impulsive behavior. When he pridefully took a census of land, for example, he was typically overreaching his mandate from God. Wimmer's problems with the Benedictine Sisters and with some of his own confreres seem to derive from this kind of impulsive self-confidence. This does not exonerate him entirely but it puts these controversies into a context that is compatible with his many admirable qualities.

We live today in a period of vibrant theological discourse. Vatican Council II was far from boring as it dealt with issues that touch the very heart of Christian experience: a reformed liturgy, collegiality,

openness to other religions and to the modern world. There was nothing defensive about this Council. Wimmer's action-oriented theology based on a prayerful faith would feel quite at home in this atmosphere with all its difficult challenges.

Monasticism without Apologies

Monasticism has an important ascetical dimension but it is primarily a witness to gospel values. It affirms the reality of divine presence in Jesus Christ and celebrates that presence in regular prayer. The image of God found in all human beings is honored, first of all, in love and respect for other members of the monastic community, and this honor is then extended in love and service to all men and women. Authentic monasticism has always been apostolic; it has always sought to share its treasures of spiritual wisdom and human knowledge with all humankind.

It has been noted with justice that Wimmer's monastic formation was rather sketchy. In the early days of Metten Abbey's restoration there was probably much that was makeshift. However, Wimmer was a well-educated and well-read man and the suggestion that he did not really understand monasticism seems quite arbitrary. This charge was made against him throughout his career as abbot and is still heard today. Specifically, he was accused of sacrificing monastic values for the sake of his single-minded devotion to missionary activities. Wimmer would probably be the first to admit that monastic observance suffered from the constant bleeding of his community for the sake of new foundations. However, that does not mean that anything essential was lacking. His monastic observance was fruitful in spiritual benefits because it did not spend its energy in preoccupied self-measurement against the theoretical ideals of others.

The Romantic Temptation

Human attitudes toward life can range from the illusion of the very romantic to the cynicism of the very realistic. There is little doubt that Wimmer's attitude was on the realistic side. He was remarkably down-to-earth and pragmatic. When some of his monks criticized his monastic observance and listened to the siren song of Beuron or Gethsemane, he concluded that they were being attracted to a form of monasticism which, though beautiful, was more out of touch than his own practical and pastoral approach.

From a romantic perspective, appearances acquire a special importance. This attitude is a constant temptation in religion because to create appearances is much less costly than to achieve true and painful interior conversion. It is easier to look like a monk than to be one.

Wimmer was not one to be greatly concerned about appearances.
If there ever was a picture worth a thousand words, it is the
photograph of Wimmer, seated with his capitulars, his skullcap slightly
off-center, behind a table whose cloth cover is all askew. This image is
an apt metaphor of his concern for substance and results rather than for
an external patina of order or charm.

A romantic monasticism looks for the glamor of soaring
towers, bucolic setting, lilting chant and flowing robes. It is not that
these are unmonastic in themselves. The danger is that they may be
given a priority over hard work, personal generosity and patient fidelity.
Wimmer certainly appreciated good music, beautiful art and fine
architecture. But, most of all, he cherished a generous heart, a steady
and reliable obedience and a deep pastoral sensitivity for the needs of
others. His monasticism was not sophisticated but it was very fruitful.

There is little evidence that those who criticized him found a better way to render Christian service or to be a witness to monastic hope.

God's Best Opportunities Are Revealed in Plain History

One of the most striking manifestations of Wimmer's commitment to gospel ideals and authentic monastic tradition was his ability to look for God's gift in the reality of life as it unfolds, rather than as it is planned or contrived. He took what life offered him and made the most of it. He did, of course, have a general vision of missionary work for German settlers in the new world but the realization of those hopes took surprising turns as history offered him both unexpected opportunities and sobering disappointments. The parish at Saint Vincent was not really a German settlement, but he chose it over the very German but less promising Carrolltown. Conventional wisdom maintains that monasteries should avoid cities, but Newark was the proverbial exception. There were very few Catholics in the South, but the poverty and need there could not be ignored. He came to care for German Catholics, but he promoted a Bohemian parish in Chicago and an Irish foundation in Iowa.

Wimmer was not wedded to any rigid plan and therefore he could accept disappointments cheerfully and seize opportunities gratefully. Like King David, he was so sure of God's goodness that he could trust his instincts; in his own way, he too leapt and danced before the ark of the covenant (2 Sam 6:14), and he too was criticized for his boldness. He allowed the American mission field to tell him what was needed and he responded with enthusiasm. As a result, he found beautiful flowers in God's meadow and he did not complain because he happened not to know the names of some of them.

Unpolished Diamonds

God certainly provides an abundance of obvious gifts in this world but the best gifts are wrapped in mystery. We all prefer the obvious, beautifully wrapped gifts but we must avoid the tragic mistake of accepting only these comprehensible favors and ignoring or rejecting the gifts that come in plain brown wrappers.

God gave the people of Galilee a Messiah who would give them what they wanted: miracles, exorcisms and glowing promises. But then God gave them a mysterious Messiah who spoke in parables and lost his power and was put to death. Only those who could accept and embrace this mysterious Messiah were able to witness and enter into the ultimate gift of resurrection glory.

Wimmer was blest in many obvious ways. But there were ambiguous and mysterious gifts in his life too. They came mostly in the form of talented but unpredictable fellow monks. Time and again he gave positions of trust to men who turned against him. They reported him to Rome; they concocted small conspiracies; they even led some away to supposedly greener pastures. The fact that they were disappointments to Wimmer is not however the real story. What captures one's attention is Wimmer's willingness to forgive them and to entrust new and greater responsibilities to them: Zilliox became abbot of Newark Abbey; Moosmueller was offered the abbot's office at Belmont; Hintenach was allowed to stay on as prior at Saint Vincent and later succeeded Wimmer as archabbot.

Wimmer was so confident that he was doing God's work that he could make the most of imperfect situations and draw the best from resistant collaborators. He would have concurred completely with the comment of one of his successors as archabbot. When Denis Strittmatter was criticized once for not leading Saint Vincent to greater achievements,

he replied simply: "I only have the cards that were dealt to me, and they're not all aces." The test of a true leader, and an expert card player, is the ability to make the most of less-than-perfect resources. Anyone can play the aces. Wimmer did not sit and complain about the cards that were dealt to him but was able to rise above hurt feelings and to challenge talented people to be productive in spite of his own and their human failings.

Trust Crowns a Faithful Life

Boniface Wimmer was a man of sturdy constitution and exceptional energy. His psychic balance was also manifested in his ability to remain calm and even-tempered in the most stressful circumstances. But it was especially his spiritual strength that emerged as his physical powers began to weaken. He was realistic to the very end: "I am afraid of death, but likewise of a long life, since it is very doubtful that I could or would do much better."

His trust in the goodness of God, which had enabled him to be optimistic in the days of his strength, became even more evident as he approached the end. He reflected: "I am therefore not sad, nor do I feel discontented or unhappy. Human beings are human beings, and suffering is suffering." It is especially difficult for strong and forceful people to deal with weakness. Wimmer had been very strong, and at the end he was very trusting in God's goodness and mercy. Trust does indeed crown a faithful life.

The accomplishments of Wimmer speak for themselves. Commenting on these achievements shortly after his death in 1887, *Sadlier's Catholic Directory* would say of the Saint Vincent Benedictines: "Nothing in the growth of the Church in this country exceeds the wonderful development of this community." The *New York Herald* commented about Wimmer: "His acts of kindness and of charity extended to all classes and conditions of society, and there is scarcely a poor family in all the region about the monastery that, at some time or another, has not been the recipient of his bounty."

Those who question the direction set for the future by the founding community may, after more careful thought, discover in Boniface Wimmer's heritage the daring wisdom and goodness needed to face the unique challenges provided by the dawn of a new millennium.

Demetrius R. Dumm, O.S.B.

"The love of Christ must come before all else. You are not to act in anger or nurse a grudge. Rid your heart of all deceit. Never give a hollow greeting of peace or turn away when someone needs your love."

Rule of Saint Benedict

The Final Word Is Love

From the road, Saint Vincent looks enormous and remote. But once we set foot within its community, we quickly discover how close it really is, and the only thing that's enormous about it is its heart.

Saint Vincent was part of my very first neighborhood. Growing up in Latrobe, I was always aware of its presence; nevertheless, the bonds of friendship are what made it real to me. Even though my family has always been Presbyterian, one of my grandfather's good friends was Archabbot Alfred Koch. My mother and father were close to Archabbot Denis Strittmatter. And Douglas Nowicki and I were friends long before he became the present archabbot—so the tradition continues. I certainly hope that my sons and grandsons will be able to know the joy of friendships with the fathers and brothers of this extraordinary Benedictine community.

Whether we talk about it or not, we human beings long to know that we are lovable, that we have value, that what we most deeply hope for is real. We want to be sure that the madness of violence, greed, hatred, even death itself is not the final word of our existence.

We long to know that the final word is Love. God gives that Word for all of us who will receive it... through lasting friendships, through the trust of children, through the beauty and power of art and science, through forgiveness, through comfort in sorrow, through hospitality to a neighbor, and ultimately through Jesus the Christ our Lord.

For 150 years Saint Vincent has been helping its neighbors to understand and to experience God's Word. May it continue to grow from strength to strength and to share its hope and heart with our world which needs more than ever what Saint Vincent has to give.

Fred M. Rogers

A Benedictine College

On Monday evening, April 11, 1994, the provost of Saint Vincent College,
Brother Norman Hipps, O.S.B., addressed a Student Government
Association assembly about a number of issues facing the school.
The audience, composed of almost a hundred faculty members and
students, listened to comments concerning grading, tuition, athletics,
violence, dormitory expansion, and development. As he summed up his
remarks, Brother Norman produced a pocket edition of the Rule of
Saint Benedict, and read the following lines from the Prologue:

Therefore we intend to establish a school for the Lord's service. In drawing
up its regulations, we hope to set down nothing harsh, nothing burdensome.
The good of all concerned, however, may prompt us to a little strictness
in order to amend faults and to safeguard love. Do not be daunted
immediately by fear and run away from the road that leads to salvation.
It is bound to be narrow at the outset. But as we progress in this way of
life and in faith, we shall run on the path of God's commandments, our
hearts overflowing with the inexpressible delight of love.

The very fact that such a sixth-century document could be read to
a post-modern generation is in itself remarkable. But just as remarkable
is the ease by which a monastic rule was adapted by the provost to an
academic mission. The assembly listened intently, evidencing a quiet
sense that this was somehow foundational to their academic lives and
human formation. The silence and then the ovation which followed
were a sign of their reaffirmation of a fundamental orientation of Saint
Vincent College as Benedictine.

Saint Benedict's description of a monastery as "a school for the Lord's service" renders it a fitting center of spiritual education so congenial for the emergence of analogous schools of intellectual life. The inscription over the entrance of Wimmer Hall echoes this theme from the Rule: "Come, children, and hear me; I will teach you the fear of the Lord." Teaching is the mission of Saint Benedict in his "school." Likewise, he regards the abbot as an instructor whose teaching "should, like a leaven of divine justice, permeate the minds of his disciples." Education as a model for spiritual and communal formation is so suffused throughout Benedict's Rule that it quite naturally develops into a primary Benedictine mission. Benedict's frequent allusions to the monks as "students," "beginners," and "children" provide the monastery with a keen appreciation of the profound potentiality of the young to learn and be formed: "Every age and level of understanding should receive appropriate treatment."

If the education model was valuable to Benedict to elaborate the character of a monastery, then it is likewise true that the model of the monastery provides the Benedictine college with a special character as well. A monastery is a community of the most intense and encompassing nature, where the temporal and social unity of a group is confirmed by a spirit of vocational and prayerful union. Placed in the heart of an educational institution which revolves around it, the monastic communion becomes a source of community and identity for many others.

The prayers of the monastic community of Saint Vincent have long provided a basic and intimate component of the college which shares its name. When parents of students are ill, when a maintenance worker is hospitalized, when a faculty member's family is grieved, or when exam-time pressures increase, requests for prayer flow readily to the monastery, are posted on its bulletin board, and are raised up in the petition of its community prayer. When death brushes one of the families of Saint Vincent's outer circle, its inner circle gathers and seals the

moment with an invocation for divine mercy. This is a rite for which the college community feels an entitlement, and a feature of social life that binds it together in a unique way.

On a more organic level, the monastic community supplies not only an intellectual and administrative resource for the college, but also an anchor of persons committed for the long haul to its students. The peculiar vow of monastic stability gives to the Benedictine college a long memory and a profound sense of continuity across several generations. Saint Vincent alumni touch base with the past, and comprehend the present state of the college by inquiring of the succession of monks who served there. "When did Father Armand die?" "Does Father John still teach anthropology?" "Is Father Earl back in Admissions?" "Who is the new moderator in Aurelius Hall?" Students who do the annual telethons realize this reality very forcefully when their conversations with alumni invariably turn to such questions.

Furthermore, the Benedictine charism of Saint Vincent College includes all members of the academic community. Laypersons comprise two-thirds of the faculty and are partners with Benedictines in accomplishing the mission of the college. Saint Vincent is a college of tutorial pedagogy, where professors are commonly perceived to be so committed to the project of student formation that they can be prevailed upon to linger after class, extend office hours, participate in student events, and offer counsel in the vicissitudes of youth. Lay and monastic faculty members alike feel the weight of the truth which is so critically Benedictine: education succeeds only within a grand investment of care and personal interest.

Such investment of care may be associated with Christ's own care, or with doing the work of God in the world. Faculty members may share these sentiments, or perceive their investment within the broad university tradition of mentoring—making real the solicitude of their *Alma Mater*, their caring mother. But even this tradition of mentoring is itself a legacy of an epoch when schools were the province of monasteries. Education was an act of adoption into a community in order to learn from a loving teacher. Saint Benedict says of the abbot and, by extension, to the teacher in a Benedictine college:

The abbot must always remember what he is and remember what he is called, aware that more will be expected of a man to whom more has been entrusted. He must know what a difficult and demanding burden he has undertaken: directing souls and serving a variety of temperaments, coaxing, reproving and encouraging them as appropriate. He must so accommodate and adapt himself to each one's character and intelligence that he will not only keep the flock entrusted to his care from dwindling, but will rejoice in the increase of a good flock.

Mark Gruber, O.S.B.

aud̄are te uirgo sacrata. De
. . . uirtutem . . . hoc ab t
os. Orõ . . . Collecta.
. . . oncede nos . . . ulos tuos
. . . mus domine de3 perpetua
. . . tis et cor . . . . falute gaudere
. . . iola b . . . ne . . . . . . Semp uirg
. . . cessione a presenti libe
. . . ctas et futura pfrui leti
. . . min

Incipiunt septem psalmi penitentiales

Domine ne in
furore tuo argu
as me: neqz in
ira tua corripi
as me. Mise
rere mei dñe
quoniam infirmus sum sana me dñe
quoniam conturbata sunt ossa mea.
Et anima mea turbata est ualde.
sed tu dñe usqzquo. Conuertere
dñe et eripe animam meam saluum
me fac propter misericordiam tuam.
Quoniam non est in morte qui
memor sit tui in inferno autem quis
confitebitur tibi. Laboraui in
gemitu meo lauabo per singulas noc
tis lectum meum lacrimis meis stra

Fire Near Saint Vincent Archabbey

We arrive with the long snow
on foot, our eyes the only light,
tracks of the last sled, our path
back to the road. Ahead the lake

where we strike the match.
The wind stales the cold rush of smoke.
The water comes easy off the flame,
and for a moment, a fire
builds in our hands. We become inhabitants.

We would leave but the monks say
fire near the road brings scholars in
to breed, to build the clearing up
into camps. A fire loses ground to ignorance,

the usual ash and stone. But we are civilized.
We forge embers out of wind. We shape footprints
to survive us, to freeze the river in
where our bodies warmed this altar,
our eyes an offering, a lasting flame.

James Ragan

The Saint Vincent Touch

Reflection on Meaning

For a quarter century, Saint Vincent has been an experience of defining importance to me as a person, a lecturer in religious studies, and a rabbi. There are the unforgettable events: when one of the nuns (pre-food service days) prepared a separate plate of food for me because she noticed that pork, a religiously prohibited food, was on the menu; a weekly lunch-time dialogue between a priest and a rabbi which began as a faith-to-faith encounter and turned into an exceptional friendship; recollections of students' comments which make me grateful to be a teacher… "I have become stronger in my Christian faith through having taken your course"… "You taught me more about the nature of the Hebrew Bible than I have learned anywhere else"; gathering evergreen branches from around Saint Vincent to cover the harvest booth erected in my backyard in celebration of the Jewish Feast of Tabernacles. Saint Vincent has been and continues to be a blessed opportunity to learn, to teach, and to practice the art of growing in mind, in spirit, and in person.

Jason Z. Edelstein

"I am absolutely persuaded
that a monastic school which
does not give just as much
attention to art as to knowledge
and religion is a very imperfect
one and that a deficiency in
scholarship at the beginning
can be more readily excused
than a neglect of art."

Boniface Wimmer, O.S.B.

Saint Vincent Seminary

On March 18, 1847, Bishop Michael O'Connor of Pittsburgh ordained Father Charles Geyerstanger, the first priest-graduate of Saint Vincent Seminary. Since that day nearly 2,300 diocesan and religious priests, including 28 bishops and archbishops, have been ordained from Saint Vincent. These graduates have exerted considerable influence in Church and society through their teaching and writing, but most of all as priests serving in numerous parishes throughout the country.

The mission, curriculum, and programs of the Seminary reflect the principles which Pope John Paul II expressed shortly after the 1991 Synod on Priestly Formation in his Apostolic Exhortation *I Will Give You Shepherds*. Saint Vincent is a member of the ecumenical Association of Theological Schools and is aware of the importance of a global vision. Over the last decade we have established programs and offered special courses to prepare priests for Hispanic ministry, rural ministry, and ministry to African-American Catholics. While the Seminary continues to focus its mission primarily on preparing priests, it also offers programs in monastic studies and programs for laypersons who seek deeper formation in their faith and are preparing for other ministries in the Church.

One cannot think about the Seminary today without reflecting on the significance of its founder, Archabbot Boniface Wimmer. It was he, for example, who from its earliest years began the custom of sending monks to the best universities in Europe and America to prepare them for teaching at Saint Vincent. As I reflect on the vitality of the Seminary and the contributions of its graduates, I am grateful for the tradition of learning that it has maintained. Most alumni can talk about a professor who has had a determinative impact on their lives: Father Baldwin, Father Oliver, Father Maurus. When I was a student Father Paulinus and Father Demetrius formed in me an appreciation for scholarship which carried over into my doctoral studies at the University of Louvain and beyond.

Even though Wimmer did not leave behind a comprehensive statement about the formation of students for the priesthood, his character and spirit continue to shape the life of the Seminary. I have selected a few key elements from Wimmer's life and his writings which I consider vital to his vision, not only in founding the Seminary but for priestly formation at Saint Vincent today. Perhaps it is Wimmer's unpretentious no-nonsense directness which gives these elements cogency and makes them a living heritage for us.

Saint Benedict teaches in his Rule that monks should "prefer nothing to Christ." For Wimmer, too, the center of a seminarian's and priest's life should be faith in Jesus Christ. In a letter to young candidates who were wavering in their resolution to accompany him to America, Wimmer wrote: "You must become [priests] only to be united to Jesus Christ more closely, to follow Him more faithfully, to do more for Him and, if necessary, to suffer and endure more for Him..." Later in the same letter: "If these are your sentiments, you will never have cause to regret having followed me when you are once in America. For you are not in quest of beautiful surroundings, a comfortable home, a life of ease, but you are seeking an opportunity of carrying the cross of self-denial after the crucified Jesus to save and regain souls..." Wimmer knew from his own experience that only a steadfast faith can triumph over the inevitable trials, disappointments and failures that a new priest would encounter. To young candidates who were about to join him in his mission to America: "I do not know the future; I have nothing to show you but the cross. 'Behold I send you as lambs among wolves,' said Christ to his disciples. He said it to us also, and I say it to you: if you are afraid of the wolves, if you fear their howling and their teeth, then stay home."

A second thing that Wimmer would say to seminary students is that they must commit themselves wholeheartedly to the mission of the Church. For him, doing God's work in meeting the needs of people and bringing the gospel to them, regardless of personal cost, seem to have been the driving force of his life. Wimmer was a man of prayer trusting in divine grace, but he knew that prayer must be combined with work.

Wimmer, a man of faith, a man of the Church, was also a man who was fully human. He responded to a situation with his whole being, and I believe his personality is somehow part of the enduring spirit of Saint Vincent. Learning of the hardships of German Catholics in America, he wrote that he was moved by "deep compassion and a desire to do something to alleviate their pitiable condition." There are many indications that Wimmer was a man of deep faith and spirituality, yet he did not go about with a solemn face. One monk who thought that Saint Vincent ought to become more like a Trappist monastery complained that the abbot was "always in the kitchen where he laughs and jokes about everything." Toward the end of his life when his own health was failing, his concern did not turn inward to his own welfare. After visiting new foundations that were experiencing difficulties, Wimmer remarked, "My chief occupation of thought and concern is for the new establishments in the South." In regard to his own health he said, "Soon there will be no place further to go. But then, I am cheerful in the Lord, and on the whole am still quite well for my age."

Finally, Wimmer believed that the education of students for the priesthood would best be accomplished on the same campus with a college where other students would be preparing for professions in many fields, and where a variety of recreational and educational opportunities would be available. Since the education of priests must be broad in order for them to understand the values and interests of people, seminarians may take elective courses in the College. The campus offers art exhibits, films, lectures by nationally-known scholars, plays and concerts by professional performers, and, above all, the resources of an excellent library.

Boniface Wimmer's challenge to students preparing for their ministry as priests is simple: Believe in Jesus Christ, and prefer nothing to Him. Commit yourself to the mission of the Church. Be yourself, a truly full human being. And get a good education. Boniface Wimmer continues to challenge Saint Vincent Seminary today, not only its students, but faculty and administrators as well.

Thomas Acklin, O.S.B.

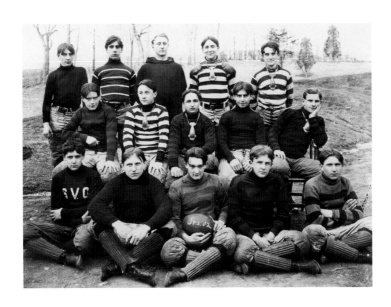

Saint Vincent Memories

I entered Saint Vincent Seminary in September 1946. This was not my
first acquaintance with Benedictine monks. I grew up on the North Side
of Pittsburgh and the first priests I really knew were the Benedictines who
staffed Saint Mary's Parish on the North Side. It was in that parish that
I made my First Communion. Benedictine priests were my first confes-
sors. It was in that parish that I attended Sunday Mass and was cate-
chized. It was for me *the* Church. The monks were, for me, holy men,
albeit somewhat mysterious. Coming to Saint Vincent was not traumatic.
I just saw a lot more Benedictine habits than I did in the parish.

　　　One of the first impressions I had of Saint Vincent was the importance
of the role that the Benedictine monks played in bringing the Gospel of
Jesus Christ to this part of God's Kingdom. I was impressed by the beauty
and care given the liturgy. It was uplifting to see a large community of

monks, clerics and novices chanting the Divine Office. Major ceremonies were major ceremonies. Sunday Solemn Vespers were made more solemn with the deep, bass voice of Archabbot Alfred intoning in German-accented Latin the *Pater Noster*.

One Pentecost Sunday we had super-Solemn Vespers, all in Latin. Monks were all over the sanctuary in various liturgical vestments. There was lots of good music and clouds of incense. It also happened to be Mother's Day. As I left the church, I heard a woman tell her companion, "They certainly do Mother's Day up right, don't they?" I said not a word.

I learned to appreciate the many ministries of gifted monks. They taught in the college, in the seminary, in the prep school. They served in parishes, and, at times, I even wondered if I should join the community.

At that time of my life, I would never have believed that someday I would be the bishop of the diocese which has Saint Vincet Arch-abbey as one of its treasures. During my seminary days, the Diocese of Greensburg did not exist. I wondered if I would ever be ordained. The thought of being bishop never entered my mind.

But when the Holy Father appointed me the third bishop of Greensburg, one of the thoughts that immediately came to mind was that I would have the wonderful opportunity of working more closely with the abbots and monks of Saint Vincent Archabbey. They are esteemed friends and co-workers. Their presence in the Diocese of Greensburg is a blessing. Archabbot Douglas was a valued co-worker when we both served the Church of Pittsburgh.

Many of the monks whom I knew have followed Boniface Wimmer into eternity. But I remember them all as having had a great impact on my life. Father Nepomucene was gruff and stern, but probably loved us in his own way. He inspired holy fear. Father Blaise, kind and gentle, would repair rattling windows while we were taking a philosophy test. In the front of my philosophy book a previous student had written, "Father Oliver goes down deeper, stays down longer and comes up drier than anyone we know." Father Ralph brought music to our ears. Father Quentin tried to pour some culture into us. Father Felix spoke about the Council of Trent as though he had been there. Father Paulinus was always generous with his time as confessor and spiritual guide. There is a rumor that he will never die.

I realize that sometimes distance lends enchantment to the view. Every day at Saint Vincent was not wonderful. Life then, as now, had good days and bad days. But one thing I know for certain. My six years at Saint Vincent Seminary and my present years as bishop of Greensburg with the Benedictine presence have had a tremendous impact for good on me. I will take responsibility for the flaws in my nature. I will give credit to the Benedictine monks for some of the good that may be in me. The spirit of Saint Benedict is alive and well in our world today because of this Benedictine community. We thank God for the blessing of their presence, their witness and their ministry.

Anthony G. Bosco

Saint Vincent Parish

1790-1846

Saint Vincent is situated on land that was deeded to John Fraser of Bedford in 1766, shortly after the French and Indian War. This land was soon to be called the Sportsman's Hall Tract because it was used for hunting. In 1790 Father Theodore Brouwers, a Franciscan friar, purchased the property and established on it the oldest continuous Catholic parish in western Pennsylvania. It was then known as Sportsman's Hall Parish. The often-pictured Sportsman's Hall structure of hewn logs was one built for Father Brouwers to serve as a residence and church.

Father Brouwers and his successors brought ministry to the Catholic settlers of this area, so much so that Sportsman's Hall Parish has been called "the Cradle of Catholicity in Western Pennsylvania." The most renowned among those early Catholic settlers in the area were the three brothers Christian, Simon and George Ruffner; and Christian's brother-in-law, Henry Kuhn. The beginnings of the Sportsman's Hall Parish coincided with the establishment at Baltimore of the first Catholic diocese in the United States, and with the installation of its first leader, Bishop John Carroll.

It was also during this time that the United States Constitution became effective with the inauguration, on April 30, 1789, of George Washington as the first president.

But Father Brouwers was at Sportsman's Hall Parish only six months until his death. His major contribution to Saint Vincent was the continuity that he ensured through his Last Will and Testament, which left the property in trust to the Catholic priest who would succeed him.

There were fifty-six years of Saint Vincent history before the arrival of the Benedictines in 1846. And these fifty-six years were rough-and-ready times for both pastors and parishioners on this frontier. A legendary pastor of Sportsman's Hall Parish was Father Peter Helbron, a Capuchin friar, who served from 1799 until his death in 1816. Through his kindness he was able to nourish a growing congregation, largely composed of German and Irish immigrants. Father Helbron, despite his advanced age, not only cared for the Sportsman's Hall Parish, but also did missionary work throughout seven counties of western Pennsylvania. He became the friend and confidant of the legendary prince-priest, Father Demetrius Gallitzin, "the Apostle of the Alleghenies."

But the development of the Sportsman's Hall Parish was given its greatest impetus in these early years by a newly ordained priest, Father James Stillinger. He served the Sportsman's Hall Parish from 1830 to 1845, and gave it a sense of community by building a brick church and parochial residence as a center of activities. It was at the dedication of this church on July 19, 1835, that Bishop Francis Kenrick of Philadelphia placed it under the patronage of Saint Vincent de Paul, whose feast day it was. From that day Sportsman's Hall Parish has been known as Saint Vincent Parish. Thus the origin of the name, Saint Vincent, which has endured to the present day as the name not only of the Parish but also of the Archabbey, Seminary and College. This Saint Vincent church was used for one hundred and twenty-eight years until it was destroyed in the fire of 1963. Those who were acquainted with Saint Vincent from 1905 to 1963 knew this church as the "Students Chapel." The walls of the parochial residence still stand as a part of Maur Hall, the oldest of the existing Saint Vincent buildings.

In 1830 Father Stillinger had been appointed not only as pastor of Sportsman's Hall Parish but also as the founding pastor of Saints

Simon and Jude Parish in Blairsville, where he served for forty-three years until his death in 1873.

In 1845 Father Michael Gallagher was appointed to take the place of Father Stillinger as pastor of Saint Vincent Parish. It would be a short pastorate for Father Gallagher, one of preparation for the coming of the Benedictines one year later. In fact Bishop Michael O'Connor of Pittsburgh successfully persuaded Father Boniface Wimmer to make his foundation of a Benedictine monastery and school on the historic Sportsman's Hall Tract. Bishop O'Connor lost little time in naming Father Wimmer as pastor of the parish; and, so as successor to Father Brouwers, he was in possession of the Sportsman's Hall Tract in accord with Brouwers' will.

The Saint Vincent of these first fifty-six years prepared the way for the arrival of the Benedictines in 1846. There had been early indications that this Sportsman's Hall Tract was destined to serve as the site for a monastery and as a center for education as well. In fact there is evidence that in 1794 the Benedictines of Downside Abbey in England had been offered by Bishop Carroll this property on which to establish a monastery and school, an offer that they did not accept. In 1835, in addition to building a church and parochial residence, Father Stillinger had a small one-story schoolhouse erected on the property. It was destined to serve as a temporary residence for Father Gallagher, and for Father Wimmer and his companions as well. This arrangement was necessitated by the fact that from 1845 to 1847 the parochial residence was serving as a temporary convent and academy for the Sisters of Mercy until they could move into a new building at an adjacent location, known as Saint Xavier Academy. Another indication of early interest in education at Saint Vincent was the attempt, also in 1845, by Father Gallagher and Bishop O'Connor to establish a minor seminary at Saint Vincent—an undertaking which was passed on to Father Wimmer upon his arrival one year later.

And so there was fertile soil in which Father Boniface Wimmer could plant the first Benedictine monastery and school in the United States. The role of Saint Vincent Parish and the Sportsman's Hall Tract was forever altered by the arrival, on October 18, 1846, of Father Wimmer and his eighteen companions. From that day Saint Vincent would be inseparably linked with the Benedictine monastery and educational institutions that would flourish on this hallowed hill.

Omer U. Kline, O.S.B.

"America is the turning point
in the history of the world."

Boniface Wimmer, O.S.B.

Saint Vincent

Reflection on the Mystery of Place

A student or visitor to Saint Vincent campus has often remarked to me about a feeling of peace that comes by stopping to reflect in a favorite spot. My favorite is the graceful row of crosses that mark the monks' resting places in the cemetery. A view of the sprawling campus from that special sanctuary evokes a symbolic and mysterious presence, and provokes in me the deepest level of feeling.

My first visit to Saint Vincent was in 1964. I have vivid recollection of coming to Saint Vincent in order to interview as part of the selection process for the architect who would design a new monastery building. Just a year and a half before, a disastrous fire had destroyed most of the monks' living quarters. Many questions flooded my mind as I was escorted through a maze of corridors and spaces. What is going on in this place? How can a monastery, a college, a parish, and a seminary all relate to each other? Is there a unity of intention? What is the fundamental attitude that I as an architect must grasp and express in the design of a new building? Does this environment help develop an awareness and a sense of caring about what a person sees and feels in this world and how one acts in this life? Should the new building be an affirmation for action, or simply a refuge from the world?

Over a period of thirty years as an architect and planner, I have come to recognize and appreciate the great diversity of people and interests that make up the Saint Vincent community. Monks and laypersons, young and old, men and women, students, faculty, administrators, and craftsmen with diverse interests—science and religion, art and architecture—all exchange ideas as part of their daily routine. A rich architectural heritage underlies this diversity. Some of the buildings which exist today were constructed by monks over a century ago with bricks made by their own hands. One senses in the architecture of those early days a simplicity of intention and a commitment to create an honest, humane environment.

I knew that the character of all new construction would have to respect and be in harmony with the authentic spirit of this heritage. For example, the new science complex, completed in 1969, could not be in conflict with the character of the basilica, completed in 1905. No conflict between the old and the new; no conflict between science and religion. Through intense interaction with many people over the years I have discovered that Saint Vincent is a human energy center, a motivating force through its people and its environment, inspiring both reflection and action. There is recognition that our world is incomplete, and often threatened by violence. In the face of this reality one senses the fundamental attitude of affirmation. Saint Vincent is not a place of despair or cynicism. It is a place of hope.

What is the responsibility of an architect in the Saint Vincent environment? First of all, planning and design must be in harmony with

the spiritual affirmation of hope. There must be a natural, effortless integration of the new with the old. New spaces must be sensitive enough to preserve, yet bold enough to proclaim. A respect of diversity, a respect for land and sky and trees. Not a mindless destruction to achieve short-term goals that will gradually impoverish the human spirit. The architect must take the bold risk of defining, enclosing, protecting, and creatively building so as to enable people to celebrate the Good—and to dance without restraint. Only in this way will the people who experience the mystery of this place have confidence in themselves, and thus hope and build in the face of the incompleteness and the violence they will encounter.

As an architect whose life-vocation is to study how environment can enrich the lives of people, I have been privileged to participate in creating the ambiance of the Saint Vincent campus. New spaces are carefully woven into the fabric of the community and encourage one to live a centered life. Architecture offers a cultural bridge to expand human experience. It provides an atmosphere for a kind of astonishment that occurs when one discovers a new thought, a new view, a new space. Perhaps even a moment of illumination occurs and the need to share the secret of discovery, which then becomes a shared possession. A love of place. A love of being. There is a spiritual exchange when one is affirmed by the ambiance, and one in turn is inspired by the ambiance to affirm. In this way, learning becomes fundamental inspiration.

The architecture of Saint Vincent is part of a unique cosmos that heralds a declaration of life taking creative possession of space. It is a call to share in the world's making—to enhance what exists by the sheer power of one's presence and action. We are in awe of the mysterious truth that every woman and man is called upon—on the foundation of their own life, understanding, suffering and joy—to create and to build for us all.

Tasso Katselas

Boniface Wimmer

The Founding Story

Greeting every visitor who approaches the Saint Vincent Archabbey Basilica, a bronze statue of Archabbot Boniface Wimmer, founder of the first Benedictine monastery and school in the United States, stands prominently at the basilica entrance. In one hand is the Rule of Saint Benedict while the other hand points forward with outstretched arm. This pose aptly symbolizes the founder's gift for combining fidelity to tradition with boldness of vision.

Energized by this vision of faith, Wimmer's initial efforts have developed into a multitude of apostolates currently undertaken by monks of the Archabbey in partnership with dedicated laypersons: a college, a seminary, some 30 parishes, a priory and high school in Savannah, the Catholic Center at Penn State University, and priories in Brazil and Taiwan. Furthermore, the American Cassinese Congregation of 21 independent monasteries in North America, totaling over 1200 monks, can trace its origins largely to the creative impulse of Boniface Wimmer.

European Background

The atmosphere for Benedictine monastic life in Europe at the beginning of the nineteenth century was anything but promising. All but a handful of the hundreds of monasteries that had flourished during the Middle Ages had been suppressed. After 1820, however, a period of restoration witnessed the rise of leaders who perceived the value of reviving the monastic movement, a movement which had contributed so extensively to the formation of Christian culture on the continent. Prominent among these heads of state was King Ludwig I of Bavaria.

In 1830 the young monarch decreed the restoration of Saint Michael Abbey at Metten. This abbey, active since its founding in the eighth century, had been suppressed in 1803. The abbey came to life again in 1830 when two elderly monks returned after an absence of 27 years. Clearly the abbey could not survive without an influx of new members. The bishop of the Diocese of Regensburg approached priests of his diocese to inquire whether they might wish to join the new community.

One of the young priests who responded to the invitation was Sebastian Wimmer. Born in Thalmassing, Bavaria, on January 14, 1809, he pursued his studies at the University of Munich and was ordained a priest on August 1, 1831. Upon entering the novitiate of Saint Michael Abbey in December of 1832, he took the name Boniface and thus chose as patron saint the great eighth-century missionary apostle of Germany.

Projectenmacher

Almost from his earliest days as a monk at Metten, Wimmer placed himself at the center of action. While serving as professor at the school of the newly established Saint Stephen Abbey in Augsburg, he worked to reestablish Saint Michael's as an independent abbey. He strove to promote the establishment of a Benedictine house of studies in Millersdorf to train missionaries. His involvement in such causes earned him the rather derogatory nickname *Projectenmacher*, meaning "quixotic dreamer" or "visionary."

As early as 1842 Father Boniface began to petition his abbot, Gregory Scherr, for permission to go to America as a missionary. In May 1845, Wimmer met Father Peter Lemke, a German priest serving in Carrolltown, Pennsylvania, who, with the approval of Bishop Michael

O'Connor of Pittsburgh, had traveled to Europe to seek aid for the bishop's new missionary diocese. In Munich he met Boniface Wimmer, who thereafter was even more determined to carry out his plan to found a Benedictine monastery in the United States. After many refusals of Wimmer's repeated petitions and upon the urging of King Ludwig and the Apostolic Nuncio to Bavaria, Abbot Gregory finally gave his consent.

On July 25, 1846, Wimmer and 18 candidates for monastic life departed from Munich and, after a stormy ocean voyage, arrived in New York City on September 15. None of the 18 had received any monastic training until their leader gave them instructions about the Benedictine Rule on board ship. When they reached Carrolltown, they found the land unsuitable for farming. After a meeting with Bishop O'Connor, who offered the group property called Sportsman's Hall nearer to Pittsburgh, the band of missionaries settled at this present site of Saint Vincent on October 18, 1846. Shortly thereafter the 18 candidates were invested as monks. Thus was achieved the beginning of the first Benedictine community in the United States.

Monasticism with Heart

Despite early hardships and setbacks the community's growth exceeded anyone's expectation. In August 1847 Father Peter Lechner, O.S.B., of Scheyern Abbey in Bavaria arrived with 20 candidates for the lay brotherhood. By 1849 there were nearly 50 men in the community. The college and seminary also grew quickly. Wimmer was determined to maintain a high quality of education amidst the rigors of frontier life. His philosophy of Benedictine education has often been characterized by his own quote: "I will not spare expense to teach the students first the necessary, then the useful, and finally the beautiful things, as long as they contribute to their refinement."

Wimmer understood that a good school depended foremost on a competent faculty. He sent his monks out for studies in the best European and American universities. Two lay professors from Bavaria, who were added to the faculty in 1848, were eminently qualified in mathematics and music. The catalogue of 1859-60 could boast of a library of 12,000 volumes and a curriculum preparing students for professions in law, science, medicine, education, and business. Between 1847 and 1857 Saint Vincent received nearly 300 oil paintings from the collection of King Ludwig. In 1866 Abbot Boniface established a house of studies in Rome for

American Benedictine students. Saint Vincent Seminary, too, was soon firmly established: already by 1848 there were 25 students enrolled, with a faculty of five professors.

Saint Vincent was raised to the status of an independent priory in 1852. Then on August 24, 1855, Pope Pius IX officially promulgated an apostolic brief whereby Saint Vincent became an abbey, the first monastery of the new American-Cassinese Congregation in the United States. At the same time the Pope personally appointed and blessed Wimmer as the first abbot of Saint Vincent for a three-year term. When this temporary appointment expired, Wimmer was elected by the monastic community according to the usual Benedictine practice.

New Foundations

Soon Boniface Wimmer's vision of extending Benedictine communities throughout the United States began to show signs of fulfillment. In 1856 the abbot and monastic chapter considered requests from four bishops to establish missions in their dioceses. The monks decided first to send missionaries to the Diocese of Saint Paul, Minnesota, a region with many German settlers but few priests. A priory was established there in 1858, and in 1866 it attained the status of an abbey. This community, Saint John's Abbey, grew to be the largest Benedictine community in the world. In 1857 the Saint Vincent community responded to an appeal for help from Kansas. The original foundation of two monks expanded to become a priory in 1858 and then became Saint Benedict's Abbey in 1876. Despite his reservations about founding a monastery in a city, Abbot Boniface agreed to send monks to Newark, New Jersey, in 1857. The unique urban community became Saint Mary's Abbey in 1884.

The Saint Vincent community also felt a special responsibility for service in the American South. Monks were stationed in Kentucky, Virginia, North Carolina, Texas, and Alabama. Some of these ventures failed and the abbot had to withdraw his men. Others developed into independent abbeys, notably Belmont Abbey in North Carolina (1884) and Saint Bernard Abbey in Alabama (1891). Abbot Boniface and the community also responded to requests for Benedictine monks in Illinois and Colorado. Springing from these early foundations were Saint Procopius Abbey (1894) and Holy Cross Abbey (1925). In 1857 Wimmer remarked, "Each abbey must become the mother of other abbeys: the mission spirit does not allow me to rest nor to stand still."

The founding story of the Benedictine Sisters in the United States is also related to Boniface Wimmer and the foundations Saint Vincent had made. In 1851 Wimmer had appealed to the Priory of Saint Walburga at Eichstätt in Bavaria for sisters to teach in the settlements where he had established monasteries. The following year Wimmer helped three sisters from Eichstätt to establish a community in St. Marys, Pennsylvania. The subsequent story of his relationship with the sisters was often one of contention over the issues of authority and the allocation of funds. The matter of jurisdiction was finally settled by a Roman decree of 1859 which determined that foundations of Benedictine Sisters in the United States would be independent of Wimmer and the American-Cassinese Congregation. Nevertheless, the sisters and monks ultimately have built upon one another's work, and both groups have made significant contributions to church and society.

The Civil War caused the community anguish. Saint Vincent was cut off from its foundations in the South, and some monks were drafted into the Northern army. At various times the monastic community suffered from serious crop failures and financial debt. The 25th anniversary year of 1871 began with a financial misadventure in Kansas and ended with the destruction of Saint Joseph Priory in Chicago during the great fire in that city. Still the abbot was able to inspire the community to see promise in each crisis and to share the little they had with others. During the bank failure of 1872-73, Wimmer wrote, "We daily give food to thirty or forty strangers and shelter them in our exterior buildings." His practical theology in the face of crisis might be summed up in his comment "Man's adversity is God's opportunity."

Forward, Always Forward

Boniface Wimmer died on December 8, 1887. Despite all the setbacks and difficulties, Wimmer's 41 years of prayer and work in America had produced results. The college and seminary had prospered, now bolstered with a charter from the Pennsylvania legislature to grant academic degrees. The foundations from Saint Vincent formed a network of monastic houses and schools from coast to coast. Abbots of the foundations had received their formation under Wimmer and in many cases reflected his enterprising spirit.

Toward the end of his life he wrote, "No one imagined us capable of accomplishing anything significant, and yet we *did* accomplish something. God's grace was obviously with us..." The legacy of the indomitable spirit that Boniface Wimmer gave to Saint Vincent can be summed up in his own words: "Our customary tendency to move forward must continue. Forward, always forward, everywhere forward."

Donald S. Raila, O.S.B.

The Birth of a Butterfly

From a Protestant's Eye

In the beginning…

    St. Vincent is only a view, a lovely panorama from my home.

    St. Vincent is a cloistered place where few women dare to tread.

    St. Vincent is a New Monastery forbidden but for a few.

    A place for bread… German nuns serving food.

The beginning of the awakening…

    St. Vincent is a theater where creativity abounds.

    The Basilica provides beauty beyond my imagination… a

    Christmas splendor… a Messiah performance… an awesome

    place for weddings and funerals.

    The communities begin to blend. The panorama comes alive.

    Students, female, too, bring life to this lovely, serene

place… a place to be recognized… to be stimulated
through knowledge… through the arts.

And now…

St. Vincent is a true part of our community without losing
beauty, dignity, or purpose.

I feel a part of St. Vincent, as can all who choose to be.

I love St. Vincent and its stimulating people.

I am pleased to have experienced the birth of this beautiful
butterfly. God has blessed us all.

Diana B. Kreiling

"Therefore we intend
to establish a school for the
Lord's service. In drawing up its
regulations, we hope to
set down nothing harsh, nothing
burdensome. The good of all
concerned, however, may
prompt us to a little strictness
in order to amend faults
and to safeguard love."

Rule of Saint Benedict

Saint Vincent Prep and Saint Xavier Academy

The story of the Sisters of Mercy in western Pennsylvania connects with that of the Saint Vincent Benedictines from earliest days. We came to the newly established diocese of Pittsburgh with its first bishop, Michael O'Connor, in 1843, and in 1845 opened Mount Saint Vincent Academy for young ladies on the land where Saint Vincent Archabbey now stands. When the Benedictine monks arrived in 1846, the Sisters of Mercy moved to the Kuhn Farm property about one mile west of Saint Vincent to a new convent and school, and renamed it Saint Francis Xavier Academy.

The monks lent assistance to the Saint Xavier community from the start, celebrating Mass in the convent chapel, giving religious instructions to the academy students, and bringing the consoling presence of the church with graveside blessings at the sisters' burial in Saint Xavier Cemetery. The Prep School and Saint Xavier Academy developed a friendly association sharing scholastic activities down through the years—musical programs, school plays, debate tournaments. Saint X girls cheered at Prep sports events, and students from both schools danced at one another's dances.

Both places influenced my life beginning in the late 1940s. My family moved to Latrobe from an area of central Pennsylvania where there were very few Catholics, so Saint Xavier provided my first opportunity for Catholic education. In the summer of 1950 Father Ralph Bailey recruited a group of Saint X students to assist with cataloguing materials in the music department at Saint Vincent. My two sisters and I were among the volunteers. We passed many happy hours that summer in the environment of working-fun. During the next several years we regularly travelled between SXA and the Prep for academic, social, and spiritual events. I've heard it said that Prep graduates are among the most loyal alumni of Saint Vincent. It is not difficult to imagine why this is so when I recall the lasting impression left by monks who were teachers there in the 1940s and 50s. Many a snowy Saturday morning Father Warren Raab drove a carload of us to a debate tournament in Pittsburgh. Father Jerome Rupprecht led groups of students from both schools on field trips through the woods and marshes of Westmoreland County. Often on Saturday evenings, too, he would organize and chaperone a skating party for us at Harry's Rink in Latrobe. Father Wilfred Dumm always had a ready ear for a Saint Xavier student weighed down by some problem, and made religion classes both challenging and fun. Sometimes, too, Father Louis Sedlacko would call my dad to ask if "one of your daughters would do an act of kindness" by accompanying some shy, dateless Prep student to the Kitty Ball or prom.

Those Saint Xavier years not only cultivated my vocation to the Sisters of Mercy, but they formed a sense of Saint Vincent as a good place that remains with me to this day. While I probably could not have named it as such at age fifteen, I recognized the monks as educated men and people of faith, the teachers of Christian culture down through the ages. Years later when I came back to teach at Saint Vincent Seminary and College, that early awareness of a place grounded in a long, rich tradition returned. The Benedictines seem able to create a wholesome environment of faith, while holding religiosity and false piety at bay. I've watched it over the decades: young monks animated by a visible fervor, and older monks ennobled by fidelity in quiet and unnoticed routines; faith expressed in rare moments of good church liturgy, and faith lived in daily moments of ordinary work and prayer; scholar-monks engaged in biblical exegesis in the classroom in the morning, and monk-scholars planting trees to beautify the campus in the afternoon. Not heaven, but a blessed place, real and earthy, where grace appears persistently present.

Saint Vincent Prep closed in 1971, and a fire destroyed Saint Xavier on March 16, 1972. On the day of the fire, it was Brother Pat Lacey and the Saint Vincent fire brigade whose fast and efficient rescue efforts saved everyone, elderly sisters to young students, from harm. The neighborly community relationship begun in 1846 had come full circle.

Patricia McCann, R.S.M.

"We belong to the whole world."

Boniface Wimmer, O.S.B.

China

Benedictines from Saint Vincent Archabbey first went to China in 1925 when the country was in the midst of armed conflicts between warlords and revolutionary forces trying to unify the fledgling Republic. The Benedictines intended to begin a priory in Peking and to establish the city's first Catholic university. In 1929, with the approval of China's Ministry of Education, Fu Jen Catholic University opened its doors to Chinese students.

   This project in China had begun at the request of Pope Pius XI and was under the auspices of the American-Cassinese Congregation of Benedictines with Saint Vincent Archabbey as the primary sponsor. Over twenty Benedictines from various American abbeys, the greatest number coming from Saint Vincent, shared the work at the priory and university in these early years.

Archabbot Aurelius Stehle of Saint Vincent Archabbey was the primary moving spirit behind this Benedictine venture into China and was the first chancellor of Fu Jen Catholic University. His untimely death in 1930 and the Great Depression in the United States, however, made the continued operation of the university by the Benedictines highly problematic. In 1933 Fu Jen Catholic University was handed over to the Society of the Divine Word, who then operated the university until it was taken over by the Chinese Communist government in 1950.

In 1960, at the urging of Pope John XXIII, Archbishop (later Cardinal) Paul Yu-Pin began working for the reestablishment of Fu Jen Catholic University in Taiwan. At this time, Archabbot Denis Strittmatter sent Father Hugh Wilt, who as a young cleric and priest had been a member of the Peking endeavor, to Taiwan to assist with this undertaking.

In the spring of 1963, the Saint Vincent community under the leadership of newly-elected Archabbot Rembert Weakland approved the establishment of a dependent priory in Taiwan near the reestablished Fu Jen Catholic University. A priory building was constructed and was dedicated on the feast of Saint Boniface in June 1964. The foundation was named Wimmer Priory after Archabbot Boniface Wimmer, the founder of Saint Vincent Archabbey. It has become a center of Benedictine prayer and hospitality. The Divine Office is recited daily in Chinese. Monks from Wimmer Priory have also worked as teachers and administrators at Fu Jen Catholic University. The priory in the 1960s established a Catholic community in the neighboring town of Linkou, which is now a very active parish of Chinese Catholics. The large yard at the priory has functioned as a playground for three generations of Chinese youngsters.

At present Brother Nicholas Koss from Saint Vincent and Father Cyprian Weaver from Saint John's Abbey (Minnesota) are assigned to Wimmer Priory. A number of priests and brothers from other religious congregations are also in residence at the priory while they study Chinese at Fu Jen Catholic University. Both Brother Nicholas and Father Cyprian teach at Fu Jen. Father Cyprian is assisting with the establishment of a College of Medicine. Brother Nicholas, who teaches in the English department, has organized two international conferences on literature and religion that were held at Fu Jen (1986 and 1990) and attracted scholars from Asia and the West. He also participated in the establishment of an Asian association for the study of literature and religion.

Benedictine Sisters from Saint Benedict in Minnesota went to China in 1930 and first worked at Fu Jen Catholic University and later at Kaifeng. In 1949 the community moved to Taiwan. Since Father Hugh's arrival in Taiwan in 1960 the monks of Wimmer Priory have worked closely with the sisters in attempting to bring Benedictine life to China. The sisters and Brother Nicholas are also planning to start a program for Benedictine Oblates as well as to work on the translation of books about Benedictine monasticism into Chinese.

In recent years the Chinese Mainland has opened considerably to the outside world. At the instruction of Archabbot Douglas Nowicki, Brother Nicholas has been working with officials of the Beijing Fu Jen Alumni Association and administrators of the Fu Jen Catholic University in Taiwan towards the reestablishment of a Fu Jen in Beijing. As a first step in this direction, Brother Nicholas and other professors from the Taiwan Fu Jen will be teaching short-term courses in Beijing on the grounds of the old Fu Jen Catholic University.

As part of its sesquicentennial celebration, Saint Vincent Archabbey will host an international conference on the history of Benedictines in China and on Benedictine values and Chinese culture.

Paul R. Maher, O.S.B.

Brazil

The story of our priory in Brazil begins with the Saint Vincent community meeting of January 9, 1963. An excerpt from the minutes of that meeting reads as follows: "In regard to the Priory of Santos, many capitulars were interested...It was almost the unanimous opinion of the capitulars that this project should be undertaken as described in the last Chapter." There is an additional note that Archabbot Denis Strittmatter ended the discussion by stating that a few men would be sent to the priory during the summer of 1963.

Many monks volunteered to be part of the new community in Brazil. Archabbot Rembert Weakland, who had recently been elected to succeed Archabbot Denis, selected four of us who had volunteered, and appointed me prior. The monastery, which was now a dependent priory of Saint Vincent, had been founded in 1650. The five members of the Santos community welcomed our arrival—four German-born priests and Brother Miguel, the only Brazilian-born member.

Now, as I reflect on my experience of thirty years in Brazil, one strong feeling predominates that seems to suffuse the factual information that comes to mind. From the beginning, the Brazilian people welcomed me as brother and friend. And in turn, I have given my heart to the people of Brazil. I still recall those first days when we were still learning a new language and the misunderstandings that often brought hilarious results. After my first sermon in Portuguese, a teacher from the local high school patiently went over all the mistakes that I had made.

The monastery, Saint Benedict Priory, is located near Vinhedo, a city of 45,000 inhabitants. We are about an hour's drive from Sao Paulo, a city with a population of 17 million people. Our long-term objective

has been to establish an independent Brazilian Benedictine community at Vinhedo, which in turn would lead to other foundations.

We took several measures in order to build a solid monastic community that would enable us to focus our attention on meeting the religious needs of the people in the region. The priory had been operating a fair-sized winery and a farm when we arrived. In 1968 we voted to close the winery, and two years later we began to sell the farm. The proceeds from the sale of land enabled us to construct a monastery, which was dedicated in November 1972. The Siloe Retreat Center was inaugurated in 1975; and the church, begun in 1986, was dedicated in 1991.

Our community, with Father Cristiano Aparecido Brito as prior, now numbers seventeen, all but four being Brazilian. Six of the monks are in the formative stage of studies on the graduate or undergraduate level. More than 3,000 persons come to the retreat center annually. We do a lot of counseling work, and are challenged to provide theological formation for lay leaders of base communities which are multiplying rapidly. Some of the monks teach theology at a nearby university. In order to support our

religious mission we are also engaged in teaching English classes, translating, and growing vegetables for the monastery and retreat center.

Pentecostal and fundamentalist sects are proliferating in Brazil. Our community will have to assume a greater role in ecumenical dialogue, which at present is almost non-existent. During the 20-year military dictatorship, the vast majority of people became poorer. Our voice in support of the poor in their struggle will continue to be a major responsibility. The face of the Catholic Church in Brazil is slowly changing toward a "preferential option" for the poor.

We have made steady progress toward accomplishing our long-term goal of establishing a Brazilian Benedictine community. The prior and the majority of our members are now Brazilian. We are, however, not yet an independent priory; we continue to count on the support of the Saint Vincent community and our many American friends.

Leo Rothrauff, O.S.B.

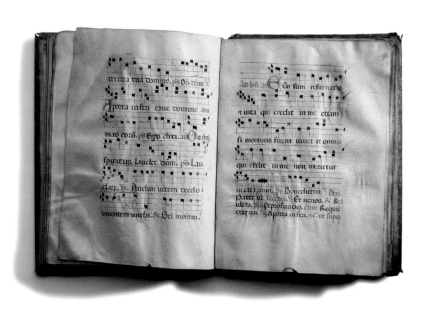

Saint Benedict

Benedict's name and tradition arrived at Saint Vincent with Boniface Wimmer and his eighteen companions. They brought with them the Benedictine way of life from Saint Michael Abbey at Metten in Bavaria and in so doing made Saint Vincent heir to a monastic tradition which stretches back to the venerable abbeys of Monte Cassino and Subiaco in Italy.

Born into comfortable circumstances at Nursia about the year 480, Benedict was sent to Rome for higher education. He left the Eternal City after only a short time, however, disturbed by the loose morals of his fellow students. Benedict established himself as a hermit at Subiaco, and once he was "discovered," monks of a nearby monastery asked him to be their abbot. His tenure with that community was short-lived, however, since he was much more zealous than they. At one point, his monks tried to poison him. Benedict returned to his hermitage at Subiaco and was joined by a number of disciples. He built twelve monasteries on the hills outside the town, and about the year 529, left the monasteries at Subiaco in the charge of others and set off with several companions for Monte Cassino. It was on those heights that he destroyed a pagan temple, established a community, and wrote his *Rule for Monasteries*. Benedict died at Monte Cassino sometime after the year 546.

These are the basic facts about Benedict's life, but one can know a good number of facts about someone without ever really knowing the person. The Benedict who is worth knowing, the author of the Rule and the subject of Book Two of the *Dialogues* of Saint Gregory the Great, was a man of flesh and blood, filled with the Holy Spirit and faith. To get to know Benedict on that deeper personal level is to meet someone whose life continues to inspire people even fourteen hundred years after his death.

Benedict was passionate for God and the things of God, and he knew that human life involves making choices which provide life with its basic orientation. In the Rule, Benedict challenges his monks to make a fundamental choice and to recognize that "the love of Christ must come before all else." He reinforces this by referring to Christ's own teaching: "First of all, love the Lord your God with your whole heart, your whole soul and all your strength, and love your neighbor as yourself."

To indicate that this choice of faith is at the heart of monastic life, Benedict expands on his passion for the things of God in the conclusion to the Rule:

This, then, is the good zeal which monks must foster with fervent love: "They should each try to be the first to show respect to the other" (Rom 12:10), supporting with the greatest patience one another's weaknesses of body or behavior, and earnestly competing in obedience to one another. No one is to pursue what he judges better for himself, but instead, what he judges better for someone else. To their fellow monks they show the pure love of brothers; to God, loving fear; to their abbot, unfeigned and humble love. Let them prefer nothing whatever to Christ, and may he bring us all together to everlasting life.

For Benedict, both Christianity and monastic life call forth what is heroic and what leads to glory. They both involve a lifelong search for God driven by passionate faith.

Benedict's zeal for God and the things of God was matched by his deep appreciation of the human person. He was humane. Gregory the Great writes of how Benedict worked his first miracle already as a youth because he was "a kind and generous-hearted boy and felt compassion for his nurse in her distress." The second chapter of the Rule is entitled "What Kind of Man the Abbot Ought to Be." It might just as well be called "What Kinds of Monks the Abbot Can Expect to

Have." Some monks will be obedient, docile, patient, upright, and perceptive; but Benedict observes that others will be undisciplined, restless, negligent, disdainful, evil, stubborn, arrogant, and disobedient. His care for this last group is remarkable. The great love of the Good Shepherd, who left the ninety-nine on the hillside to go in search of the stray, is evident when Benedict writes about how concerned the abbot ought to be for monks who deserve to be excluded from certain parts of monastic life. The abbot must exercise the utmost care and concern for wayward brothers and he ought to use every skill of a wise physician in his treatment of them. Benedict urges the abbot to act with all speed, discernment, and diligence in order not to lose any of the sheep entrusted to him because he has undertaken care of the sick, not tyranny over the healthy. Seldom does Benedict exhort the abbot as ardently as he does when he writes concerning the care which the abbot ought to exercise for these monks who are the most troublesome.

Benedict was thoroughly grounded in tradition. Indeed, because he was rooted in tradition, he was able to do something new. When he received the monastic habit from the monk Romanus, Benedict joined himself to a tradition formed by the Bible, the Catholic Church, and the monastic movement. Much of the Benedictine Rule is made up of quotations from or allusions to the Scriptures, and monks are to read the orthodox and Catholic fathers at their common prayer. Benedict relied on *The Rule of the Master* and great monastic authors such as Basil, Augustine, and Cassian. Nonetheless, even though monastic life had already flourished in the church for over two hundred years and various monastic rules had already been written, Benedict wrote his own. The new conditions which he found in sixth-century Italy called for a new response. Benedict's appropriation of the Christian monastic tradition obliged him to do something original.

Saint Benedict did great things, but he probably did them very unconsciously. He could hardly have envisioned establishing a tradition that would spread to continents which he never knew existed. At the conclusion to the Rule, he encourages his monks to keep the little rule which he wrote for beginners. Yet through this "little rule" and the passionate faith which it embodies and inspires, Benedict has shaped our civilization and touched our lives.

Kurt J. Belsole, O.S.B.

"The concern must be whether
the novice truly seeks God
and whether he shows eagerness
for the Work of God,
for obedience and for trials."

Rule of Saint Benedict

A Tribute to the Sisters

The Benedictine Sisters were a beloved part of the Saint Vincent community and were responsible for food service from 1931 to 1987. The first group of sisters arrived at Latrobe on February 25, 1931, under the leadership of Mother Leonarda Fritz. By 1939 forty sisters had come to Saint Vincent from their convent of Saint Walburga at Eichstätt in Bavaria.

The character of Saint Vincent today owes much to the loving presence of the sisters for so many years. They cooked and served meals, canned food and made preserves, made vestments and ceramics, knitted afghans and booties, prayed and sang. They taught us all—we were all their students—that love and good humor transform work, and make every work a personal gift.

During World War II the sisters were prevented from sending money back to their motherhouse at Eichstätt. As a consequence they were able to purchase property near Greensburg, Pennsylvania, where they established Saint Emma Monastery. In May 1987 the sisters closed their convent at Saint Vincent and moved to Saint Emma, where they continue their ministry as a thriving retreat center.

In 1989 Saint Vincent honored the sisters through a Founders Day Exhibit at the King Ludwig Gallery on campus. The program of the exhibit was titled "Saint Vincent's Gentle Touch: The Benedictine Sisters." All who have been privileged to know them are grateful for the abiding influence of that loving "gentle touch." In a true spiritual sense the sisters will always be a beloved part of Saint Vincent.

Douglas R. Nowicki, O.S.B.

The Benedictine Sisters

They Also Teach

No longer able to work,
The old sister
Sits praying for us all
And dozing.

In her sleep,
She drops her beads;
But her gnarled old hands
Still move in two familiar patterns:
They pull the missing beads
And then they move
Back and forth,
Still peeling potatoes,
Her work of over fifty years.

At night, though,
She often stirs.
The other sisters hear her
In her sleep
Encourage a sister, long dead.
"Mach schnell, Schwester.
Hurry up!
Mother Leonarda told us:
The boys are sick;
Make them soup;
Mach schnell."

After the sisters' meals,
She pushes her walker; and
Barely able to hold the rag,
She cleans the tables after them.
She cannot work now
So she prays
For all of us
And dreams of Him.

Richard Schulte

Outrageous Hope

He planted trees. Told he had but six months or so to live, he planted trees.
I wondered why he didn't plant flowers—he'd get to see them bloom.
Or why not spend time in prayer and study, steeling his spirit for death?
Now, over twenty years later, as I pause on my way to class, looking out
the window over the tops of the lindens and ornamental pears he planted,
I think I know. I think of Jeremiah planting trees, trees that would take
years to bear first fruit, even as he prophesied the imminent destruction
of Jerusalem and Judah—I think of Jeremiah: what extravagant faith,
what outrageous hope. What a gift he left us, in these trees planted all
around us and in this garden I now look out over, a garden named
"Melvin Platz" in memory of Father Melvin Rupprecht.

As I think of my students waiting for me, these trees seem an
obvious metaphor for the teaching vocation. Many have written about

how plumbers and electricians know rather quickly—turn a valve, flick a switch—whether or not they have been successful, while teachers only rarely see their successes or failures, the results are so far off in time and distance. Yet we are Jeremiahs, Father Melvins, nurturing faith and hope in our hearts that the trees will mature, and so on we toil.

Perhaps a less obvious metaphor embodied in these trees, however, is that of *teachers* as trees. On this sunny day, I think of a note I recently received from Tim Zadai, class of '68. In it, Tim recalled how disappointed he was with the grade I had given him on his first essay in freshman writing. Yet he felt encouraged to do better in my course, encouragement that he told me led him to continue working to improve his writing at Saint Vincent and later in both graduate school and career. That's the "student-as-tree" metaphor, but I am thinking more about what Tim included with his note—a photocopy of that first essay, an essay written for the first class I taught at Saint Vincent. So Tim's essay was the first I ever assigned, and among the first I ever corrected and graded. I watch white clouds light the sky behind Kennedy Hall and recall with a wry smile the folded photocopy Tim sent, its few sparse and fussy grammatical corrections, its cursory final comment, its over-confidently written C minus, and see it now as a measure of my growth as a teacher, for I find in it (my "freshman essay" too) an assignment that I would not think of giving to freshman students today, corrections and comments I would not make today, and the absence of comments I should have made. We've grown together here, these trees and I, students and colleagues, and Penny and Ryan, my family.

In the fall of 1990, when I was lucky enough to be awarded a national bronze medal in the CASE/Carnegie Foundation's 1989 Professor of the Year program, I told Brother Norman, College Provost, that I felt I would not have received such an award had I been a teacher at a college other than Saint Vincent. I arrived at Saint Vincent a lapsed Methodist at a time of religious and spiritual ferment on campus right after the Second Vatican Council. Saint Vincent turned out to be important in the formation of my Christian faith. A little later, students and faculty concerned about social justice led me to make a commitment to the world's hungry people: I've done anti-hunger work with government, secular, and ecumenical agencies and with Redstone Presbytery for almost twenty years now, and in a sabbatical year in 1980-81 worked as Hunger-Action Enabler for the Synod of the Trinity (Presbyterian Church USA). These gifts of the College were pivotal in my career.

Saint Vincent also gave me the encouragement and the means not simply to teach students, but to learn from them too. When Father Maynard, then College President, rehired me for my second year, he gave as his most important reason that I "frequently had been observed talking with students outside of class"—how telling of priorities that shaped me here. Bill Snyder, '73, an English department colleague, has named the characteristic mode of teaching at Saint Vincent "accompaniment"— faculty here accompany students in learning. I think that that accompaniment is the true Benedictine character of Saint Vincent.

Our alumni and alumnae have achieved remarkable things in life, many of them beyond all that seemed possible when they were students. Ask most from the forties and fifties about how that happened, and they will tell you that a monk came to awaken them before class when they were freshmen, or worked extra hours to tutor them, or did something special to help them through a crisis—gave what our college bulletin used to call a "personalized education." Ask later alums, and they'll tell you the same story, naming with real warmth both monks and lay faculty who gave them time, caring, and concern far beyond the required.

Finally, I think these trees, as well as Father Melvin's planting them, are a metaphor for Saint Vincent itself. Another element of the Benedictine character of the place is its slowness to change. Ten years after graduating from college, I returned to my *alma mater* to find it changed— not only its buildings and campus, but the very essence of the college. I doubt that most who return to Saint Vincent feel that way. Change takes its good old time here, and some changes never happen—for example, in the sixties, when almost all colleges, even Harvard, were abandoning required liberal arts courses, our faculty *added* courses to our liberal arts core curriculum. Our slow evolution at times is frustrating to administration, faculty, and students alike, but also it is a conserving force, like the slow growth of trees which gives them long life. I look out over Father Melvin's trees, remembering students and colleagues now departed, and think the trees might symbolize something important about us: our history is less important than our heritage, a living tradition of extravagant faith and outrageous hope.

Now I'm ready for class, eager even after all these years: I'm sure the students will be ready for me, too. It's early April: the seniors are restless; the trees in Melvin Platz grow upward toward the light, their branches spiked with buds about to break into leaf yet another year.

Ronald E. Tranquilla

They Brought You
Their Sick

Brother Cancer came to live with me in the monastery about five years ago. He arrived with an unexpected impact to tell me how important life is, my life, where I am and as I am. Eventually I got the message. He stays around to serve me in my making the decisions that define my path. Another Brother of the same name, but no relation, rushed in unannounced last year, and for months upset all my cherished plans, before retreating. "You didn't really learn all you need to, you know," he seemed to warn, "but you'd better try again." I can't escape their lurking around, but my commitment is not to them.

Nor is it to Brother Depression, who has attached himself to me as an unwelcome companion for even longer. I wonder sometimes if he's made perpetual vows. A cumbersome burden, often in the way. He would take over if he could. "So deal with it," Life sighs. "There aren't going to be only invited guests at your party."

Jesus, they brought you their sick and their repulsive outcasts in crowds, and you welcomed them. Those whom others pushed away to the fringes drew your attention and respect. Each and every one got a healing word, a consoling touch. For once someone recognized them, affirmed their right to exist. You taught your followers to bring in the abandoned and put them in places of honor at the lavish banquet of life. And after you ministered to the hopeless and vulnerable, you went and became one of them yourself. "He saved others, but he can't save himself," people scoffed. You wept from discouragement. You sweated out your isolated agony. You bled under mistreatment. You endured public humiliation and the bitterness of betrayal, denial. But you hoped and trusted, despite temptation. You offered yourself to be lifted up, and for love of others—that's us. When you felt most alone, you were closest to us. You know us because you became like us.

And who is there to bring me to the healing pool, to the Water of Life?

Illness has brought me the deepest sense of community I have ever had. My brother monks have brought me to Jesus like those Gospel people who cared, and elbowed close to him with someone dear to them. And in our shared life and common commitment they have brought Jesus to me, healing and encouraging by their acceptance. Jesus-like, they have recognized me for what I am, and kept light in my life, while saying, "You belong in this crowd with us. Whatever is being passed out, we'll see that you get some too." From them I learn that I will belong no less if my demons impair me or if I falter in my work. I had to submit to sickness to know that (it's one way to learn). And from them good things have come to me.

Even those I have lived with and who have now gone ahead have taught me the path to follow. The old abbots, Alfred and Denis, in their peaceful acceptance of infirmity and death. Elder brothers like Ildephonse, Leopold, Valerian. Buddies like Gus/Robert, Donald, Cecil, Alexander, Maurus. My younger brothers Ian, Michael, Roman, and Jimmy. Dear Jim. Tormented and outgoing, curious, laughing, irrepressible and irreplaceable. Outrageously unconventional, hungry for love and for Christ. Life opened a plan for him in circles of many hearts. Life-threatening illness brought him into the heart of community. Sudden death took him with a shock to us all. When we were ill together, you shared your faith with me, we talked of the same hopes and fears, we laughed and wondered together. You left me grateful.

Such are my brothers, much like me, and now we look forward to being together inseparably, one eternal Day, in our Brother Christ. Then illness will have served its purpose of strengthening the ties among us. My infirmities will not pursue me beyond death, but our love will make a place for me in a perfect and complete community. Belonging here helps me believe I will belong there too.

Brice Ryan, O.S.B.

"Let them prefer nothing whatever to Christ, and may he bring us all together to everlasting life."

Rule of Saint Benedict

The Challenge of
Our Moment

Those of us who rejoice in the Benedictine tradition see a great parallel between the age of Benedict and our own. His and ours are turning points in civilization. We, as he, are witnessing a change from one system and cultural context of life to another. Whether we name our moment as the post-modern age or as the dawning of an age of individualism spawning a new barbarism, parallels with the age of Benedict are striking.

Around him Benedict witnessed the decay and darkness of a society losing its way and rapidly losing its life as well. The Roman Empire that had been the foundation of human civilization for centuries was in decline and that classic age, which is still an inspiration in so many ways today, was then in a state of total collapse.

Our own world, while rejoicing in many technological and scientific advances, continues to rush somewhat headlong to embrace a philosophy that sanctions the termination of unwanted and inconvenient human life, exalts violence and a sexual indulgence that would probably bother, if not shock, some whom we have disdainfully called savages.

Saint Benedict understood that a new Christian civilization could be built in spite of the age of darkness. This would come about by seizing upon and living that fundamental principle of *ora et labora*, pray and work. He recognized that the spiritual reality we call God's kingdom in our midst and what Augustine called the city of God would come to be only through the work of people of faith. He knew that without a constant personal communion with God nurtured by daily time in prayer, we will not have the life of God within us, the life which alone

brings us to the full stature we are meant to enjoy.

Over a decade ago, these sentiments were expressed in the declaration of the Council of European Bishops Conference as representatives of 24 episcopal conferences gathered with Pope John Paul II for ceremonies commemorating the 15th century of the birth of Saint Benedict. The bishops of Europe remind us that "the Christian faith tells us that human beings are created in the image of God, even if that image is sometimes disfigured by sin." They go on to remind us "that Jesus Christ came to set free every man and woman and to place before them in a unique way the challenge of liberty: freedom for the whole reality of human life, spiritual and physical; freedom for the whole of humanity, even those left on the fringes of society and those robbed of their human heritage."

The bishops state that "this image of humanity has influenced European culture in a very special way. It will always provide us with the fundamental basis on which to ground all human dignity." What was said by John Paul II and the bishops of Europe about the old world is equally true of the new. Even our feeblest attempts to nurture human rights, human dignity and the future of humanity all take their inspiration from the gospel proclaimed in and through Christ's Church.

As in every age, the truth today remains that prayer is our contact with God. And God's kingdom will be nearer completion when all peoples and nations are filled with the life of God given us in Christ. But it is equally true, as in past ages, that many in our world today seem to have forgotten that the fullness of our life does indeed come from God alone and the fullness of life can be communicated to us only if our lives are open to God.

So, too, is human labor truly the second important and constitutive element of human life. We hear so often today the concern that the work which so many people engage in bears little relevance to who they are both as human beings and as God's people. So many today view their work simply as a necessary evil without which they could not live comfortably, and so their labor is not an authentic and intentional contribution to the development of society or of God's kingdom or even of themselves. Likewise, others in our day value work only for the wealth which it brings them. Too few in our age appreciate the creative and life-giving value of human labor which Benedict understood.

It is no secret then that what so many are longing for and seeking today is the renewing spirit which Benedict brought to the Europe of the Dark Ages—a spirit which has been kept alive since the time of this great saint by those who follow his Rule and way of life. So many are seeking some sense of the spiritual in their lives and the principles which brought the world out of darkness and into an age formed by the gospel of Christ. It should be little surprise then that Saint Vincent, which continues this centuries-old commitment to the faith and to the service of pastoral ministry and higher education, is looked to by the Church and the communities of this region to provide active leadership in the renewal of our society.

In this post-modern age, an age that is often confused, an age that is tempted to undervalue faith and religion, prayer and human labor, an age that is described as slipping into the darkness, we today need as much as ever the light of Christ that was held high by Benedict in Europe and by Boniface Wimmer in these lands. We need to regain the vision based on the message and values of these great pastors whose zeal and labor truly altered history and brought nearer to completion the kingdom of God. We continue to need this community at Saint Vincent to bring the brilliant light of Christ to a world tempted to darkness, and to bring to this troubled age beset by conflicting voices the faith and heritage of Christ alive in Benedict—a message which can truly renew once again our society and our civilization.

Donald W. Wuerl

Coeducation

The theme of the 1983 Orientation Program "A New Beginning to an Old Tradition" began a new era in the history of the college. That fall marked the beginning of coeducation at Saint Vincent. A freshman class of 240 students, of whom 33 percent were women, enrolled. Within ten years the goal of having women represent half the total enrollment was achieved.

One hears that the transition was so successful because of wide consultation and careful planning within the community. More significant, however, was the spirit of Benedictine hospitality and community that permeates the campus. The first women students were genuinely welcomed into the college community and were invited to make themselves equal partners with the men. In welcoming the first coeducational class at the beginning of the 137th academic year, the president, Father Augustine Flood,

invited all the new members of the Saint Vincent community "to take ownership." Indeed, women students have accepted the invitation and have in turn made significant contributions in all aspects of college life.

Women, like men, are generally attracted to the college by its academic reputation. Majors in business, science, math/engineering are as popular among women students as they are among men. Female students, like their male counterparts, successfully pursue graduate studies and careers in these fields as in others.

From old photographs and from conversations with alumni, one can tell that sports have always been a big part of campus life. The college encourages all students to get involved in some sport, and only secondarily emphasizes winning intercollegiate championships. Yet athletic teams have often distinguished themselves in intercollegiate competition. Older alumni talk about the baseball teams that were good enough to play exhibition games with the Pittsburgh Pirates. The 1950 Bearcat Tangerine Bowl victory over Emory and Henry College of Virginia is still recalled by many alumni.

Women students have been successful in the college's sports programs. Interest in intramural sports has been high. Competition in women's intramural flag football has been as intense as that of the men's intramural competition. Women have also distinguished themselves in intercollegiate athletics, particularly in basketball. Women's basketball teams have won conference titles eight of the past ten years, and have participated in national championship competition for the past three years.

Women students equally with men have lent their skills to many areas of campus life: prefecting, student government, orientation programs, campus ministry, newspaper, yearbook, honor societies—in fact, to every club and organization. Women have served as student government president and have been the recipients of the prestigious President's Award for the past five years. The Campus Ministry Program has been the center of campus life because of the contributions of men and women as singers, lectors, eucharistic ministers, organizers of social activities, and as volunteers for outreach programs at Clelian Heights School for Exceptional Children and the Jubilee Soup Kitchen.

Coeducation has become so much a part of our tradition that imagining a time when Saint Vincent College was not coed is difficult. Boniface Wimmer and the other Benedictines who founded the school would be proud of this accomplishment.

Alice Kaylor

"Let us consider, then, how we ought to behave in the presence of God and his angels, and let us stand to sing the psalms in such a way that our minds are in harmony with our voices."

Rule of Saint Benedict

Benedictine and American

Clashing or Blending Values

Historians studying Catholicism in the United States will note how often our generation used words like "evangelization" and "inculturation." We were fascinated, they will say, by what happened when the values found in the Catholic tradition came into contact with other ways of understanding this world and with other traditions.

Many Catholics in Europe, not recognizing the particular characteristics of the Church in the United States, continue to see the Church here as but an extension of their own. Although the European roots of our Catholicism remained clear for many decades, distinctive American qualities have mingled with the old to form something new and unique. In this context we Benedictines rightly ask: In the history of American Catholicism is there something particular about how we have adapted to the values and traditions we found here, something that makes us different from monks elsewhere? Moreover, we ask if there is something special that we can contribute to Church and society.

Though the American mentality still had much in common with Europe when Boniface Wimmer arrived here, it had already begun to show signs that would differentiate it from its European roots. The philosophical concepts about freedom and individualism that came from the Enlightenment and that fostered the French Revolution and the War of Independence in the 18th century were accepted as positive values in the United States, even by the Church. The Catholic Church in Europe, on the contrary, was unanimous in its opposition to that movement, remembering that those ideas deprived it of its previous liberty and means of existence. Concepts such as individual rights, democratic participation in government, fair play ("taxation without representation"), and free expression of ideas were taken for granted in the new atmosphere but were still considered dangerous in European Church circles. In education the role of science and inductive reasoning from experience became commonplace in the United States. Europeans tended to remain more philosophical and speculative. New attitudes were also caused by the size and vastness of the new land that afforded unheard of opportunities for the venturesome. The frontier mentality wanted constantly to seek new horizons.

Blending the New and the Old

For Benedictines, adaptation to the new world took place rapidly. Benedictines must become indigenous at once because the vow of stability roots them in the culture and place where they build their monasteries. They belong to the local church and take on quickly the characteristics of that specific place. Furthermore, new members must come from the country and region.

In blending their old tradition with the new the monks of Saint Vincent saw at once the importance of education. Their solid Bavarian educational tradition with its emphasis on the classics and science held them in good stead. It was not by accident that Saint Vincent College became known in those fields of study. In the new surroundings the monks saw

that education was important for everyone, not just for the wealthy. Thus the monks adjusted well to the methods of the new educational systems developing in the United States and tried to add to those their own aesthetic tradition. They succeeded in blending the new and the old in their schools and in their monastic liturgies.

The spirit of rugged individualism was not just an American trait; the Bavarian founders were also strong individualists. Wimmer often had problems with priors assuming authority that was not theirs. The monks used that rugged individualism to good advantage in the founding of new monasteries whose survival required freedom to make decisions and on-the-spot adjustments. Saint Vincent sought, nevertheless, to keep community life intact over against the individualism that characterized the nation. The delicate balance between community and individual was not always easy to maintain. The demands of parochial work, with monks often living alone for long periods of time, took monks away from the communal life. In such cases Wimmer tried without much success to form small priories so that the monks could live together. The monks had brought with them from Bavaria a humane and compassionate discipline. At least in theory, Saint Vincent never abandoned the importance of community worship, communal meals and recreation, and chapter meetings. As novices continued to learn, the values of community life were extolled and, although practiced with many exceptions, never abandoned.

Schools and Pastoral Activities

Saint Vincent, it must be recalled, was founded before the monastic reforms of the abbeys of Solesmes and Beuron that sought to repudiate the school tradition and emphasize a more contemplative type of monastic life. I doubt if a more enclosed monastic style of life would have adjusted as easily and as quickly to the new American values as did the Bavarian tradition of monasticism with its schools and pastoral activities.

The new monastery in America also continued to develop the talents of its individual members to the fullest. In Europe it was taken for granted that such academic development would already have been finished when one entered the monastery. Monks in Europe did not go to major universities to specialize in various fields of study. One of the intuitive responses of American Benedictines was to value the talents of the individual and give monks the best specialized training and education.

When Archabbot Alfred Koch called me to his office in 1948 before sending me to Rome for graduate studies, he talked of the importance of good theological training. He instructed me to take the major courses

taught by the best scholars in the field but advised me not to absorb my time by taking their exams. He also instructed me to spend the first summer in France to obtain more proficiency in French and to study Gregorian chant, then to spend the second summer in Germany to make myself more proficient in that language and to study piano. In the meantime in Rome I was to take music privately, both theory and piano. "But don't let your studies interfere with your education," were his last words. He was being true to the Saint Vincent and American tradition of developing the talents of the individual.

Democratic Processes

Free expression and total participation in governance caused tensions in the monastery but did not seriously divide the community. Throughout the history of Saint Vincent monastic chapter meetings were often heated and intense. As the years went by, the power of the abbot became more and more circumscribed in the canonical constitutions as the seniors and the Chapter began to play a larger role. The Solesmes constitutions, for example, adhered closer to a literal interpretation of the Rule of Saint

Benedict and stated that the abbot was to hear everyone but then to decide what he thought best. At Saint Vincent the abbot was bound by certain decisions of the Council of Seniors, by decisions of the Chapter of those monks living at home, and for the most important decisions by the whole Chapter that included those living outside the monastery. The abbot had to persuade and could not force his personal wishes upon the community.

Democratic processes entered the monastery but never became "congregational" in practice, as happened in many mainline Protestant denominations influenced by American democratic principles. Monks disagreed with their abbots but never would have thought of eliminating the concept of abbot itself. A balance was always maintained between strong leadership and the demands of participation that the new culture postulated. Having been a member of the Council of Seniors before becoming abbot, I know how much Archabbot Denis Strittmatter, like many abbots before him, struggled with these restrictions which seemed so contrary to the text and spirit of the Rule. Because of the American influence, the style of government in an American monastery tended to be more democratic and participatory.

Prayer and Work

American culture was pragmatic and experiential. The monastery absorbed that culture. Ideological monastic theories rose and fell but none ever took hold within the Saint Vincent community. For example, every decade or so saw the introduction of ideas from the Solesmes or Beuronese reforms that would have brought the monastery into a more contemplative mode, but they were not accepted. A certain pragmatic balance between the basic ideals of the Rule and the needs of the Church was sufficient to maintain the unity of the community. There have been no major ideological splits in the community of Saint Vincent in its history.

The frontier mentality also found expression in the last century in the thrust to found new monasteries. Wimmer's missionary spirit blended well with the American frontier mentality. New foundations rapidly succeeded one another.

There were some aspects of the American culture that the monastery avoided. For example, the industrial revolution separated work from calling or vocation in life. Work for the middle class often was a drudgery and just a means of earning enough money to keep the family together. The monastery did not accept that trend. Work in the monastery was seen as a part of the monastic vocation and the way each monk contributed to the community, to the Church, and to society. Such an integration of work with the monastic ideal in the new setting is one of the finest achievements of the monastic tradition of Saint Vincent. Saint Vincent has never been known as a "contemplative" monastery, but it has never abandoned its quest for balance between prayer and work. Also, it has not lost its thirst for intellectual and artistic pursuits.

The Story is Not Ended

What contribution can American Benedictine monasticism make today, both to Church and society? The monastic experience can teach the Church that participatory processes do not destroy hierarchical structures. The Benedictine Rule in the chapter on "Summoning the Brothers for Counsel" describes the kind of wisdom that the Church today is avidly seeking. Benedict knew that the Holy Spirit speaks through all, even the Daniel or youngest in the community. He knew that the process of discerning the action of the Spirit must involve all. In my years as bishop

I can say that I learned much from my monastic experience. I enjoy and profit much from meetings of the Priests' Council and the Lay Pastoral Council. I would ask the consultors to meet every day if I could. Such bodies in the Church have yet to reach their full potential. The monastic tradition with its long history of discerning through listening to all in the community could help. A monastery like Saint Vincent is a fine example of such participatory governance.

The Benedictine ideal of a sane balance between work and prayer could contribute much to our Church and to the world around us. Our society runs at a hectic pace. Few people lead a balanced life. The need to prioritize time and weigh the values of more satisfying personal relationships over against more income are real questions for Americans today.

Education in the Bavarian Benedictine tradition has not lost its importance. In addition to the traditional interests in language, literature, history, and the arts, that tradition saw a special mission to the scientists, to those who search for the meaning of this physical universe and all life on it. Benedict saw monastic life as a search for God and that search is one that every religious person is involved in. Since so many in our day do so in pursuits that were once considered secular, such an education can help to integrate life, work, and belief. The monastic experience can be helpful in achieving such an integration.

The Benedictine tradition of doing things well, whether it be art, architecture, or music, says something to our Church in the United States today. The fascination with Gregorian chant, the desire to make retreats in a monastic atmosphere, the mystery of the Liturgy of the Hours well sung—all these express a quest for the presence of the transcendent in daily life. The relationship between the aesthetic experience and the religious one was well known to the monks at Saint Vincent and remains a part of their heritage.

The story is not ended. There will be a constant need to reflect on what is good in American culture, what is consonant with the gospel and can be absorbed into the Catholic and Benedictine tradition, and what instead clashes and is harmful. By continuing to do such reflecting monks will also contribute to the ever-changing world they live in. Such contributions are not as visible as those remembered in history like copying manuscripts or teaching people how to farm, but they are no less needed in our day.

Rembert G. Weakland, O.S.B.

Notes on the Illustrations

Bronze statue of Boniface Wimmer, O.S.B., founder of Saint Vincent Archabbey, by Ferdnando Seeboeck, 1930. *Front cover*

Lay Brothers of the monastic community and craftsmen from the area pose for a picture during construction of the Basilica, October 27, 1896. *Facing title page*

Boniface Wimmer, O.S.B., about 1870. *page 11*

A stained glass window depicting Boniface Wimmer, O.S.B., setting out from Metten in Bavaria for the New World. It is one of sixteen in the Crypt of the Basilica by Emil Frei, 1946. *page 13*

The crosses in this photograph—images of hope—are part of two long rows of crosses marking the graves of Saint Vincent Benedictines. *page 15*

Archabbot Boniface Wimmer and members of the monastic community, 1885. *page 16*

"Lamb of God," a painting above the apse windows of the Basilica by Joseph Reiter. *page 18*

Felicia R. Embry ('97) and Susan Robb ('96) on the porch of Leander Hall. *page 21*

Kevin Cordera ('95) and Carla L. Burkhart ('95) in Melvin Platz. *page 23*

"The Supper at Emmaus," an 18th century oil painting, is one of many paintings given to Saint Vincent in the 1850s by King Ludwig I of Bavaria. *page 25*

Fred M. Rogers and Archabbot Douglas R. Nowicki, O.S.B. *page 26*

The Saint Vincent Summer Theater uses the Science Center outdoor amphitheater for its after-the-show cabaret. Jim Colonna ('95) is at the piano. *page 29*

Maximilian Duman, O.S.B. (1906-1990). Father Max liked to spend his summers studying plant life in the Arctic. *page 30*

Book of Hours, written on vellum about 1450, from the Saint Vincent Library collection. *page 32*

"Neighbors Serving Neighbors," a wall hanging in appliqué by Vincent de Paul Crosby, O.S.B., 1993. *page 34*

Seminary students Joseph Reigel, Bruce Chuff, and William M. Williams, 1994. *page 37*

Why do five of the "S.V.C. Jrs. '02" players have the fancy nose guards? *page 41*

Members of the Pittsburgh Steelers during their summer training camp at Saint Vincent. *page 42*

"Saint Vincent de Paul" window in the choir of the Basilica. *page 44*

A view from the organ gallery of the Basilica during a liturgical celebration. *page 47*

A connecting bridge of the Science Center. *page 51*

The swimming pool was built through a gift of Frank and Elizabeth Resnik. *page 53*

The church of Saint Michael Abbey, Metten, Bavaria. *page 57*

Portrait of King Ludwig I of Bavaria by Langermaier, about 1826. *page 58*

View of the Basilica and surrounding buildings. *page 62*

"Adoration of the Magi," a woodcarving attributed to Cosmas Wolf, O.S.B. (1822-1894). *page 69*

Archabbot with the Council of Seniors, 1994. First row: Rene M. Kollar, O.S.B., Omer U. Kline, O.S.B., Archabbot Douglas R. Nowicki, O.S.B., Albert C. Bickerstaff, O.S.B., Demetrius R. Dumm, O.S.B. Second row: Nathan M. Cochran, O.S.B., Richard Ulam, O.S.B., Thomas Acklin, O.S.B., Gilbert J. Burke, O.S.B., Vernon A. Holtz, O.S.G., David Carlson, O.S.B. *page 72*

Henrique G. Souza, N.O.S.B., and Paulo S. Panza, O.S.B., Brazil, 1994. *page 74*

Choir book, written on parchment about 1430, from the Saint Vincent Library collection. *page 76*

Detail from a stained glass window in Benedict Hall depicting Saint Benedict as teacher with Saints Maurus and Placid. *page 79*

Joel Glover, O.S.B., Richard Michel, O.S.B., and Nathan Munsch, O.S.B., 1994. *page 81*

Hermelinde Karl, O.S.B., Mother M. Leonarda Fritz, O.S.B., Gabriele Häusler, O.S.B., Martina Gerner, O.S.B., about 1960. *page 85*

"Madonna and Child," a woodcarving by Norbert and Victoria Koehn, 1982. *page 86*

A page of a 17th century German rotula from the Saint Vincent Library collection depicting Saint Benedict and Saint Michael the Archangel. *page 90*

Mass in the Basilica, 1994. *page 96*

Dr. Doreen Blandino with students in the language lab, 1994. *page 99*

Women's volleyball, 1994. *page 100*

Men's basketball, 1994. *page 101*

Saint Vincent Orchestra, 1880. Fred Moleck ('61) in his doctoral dissertation describes the rich early tradition of music at Saint Vincent. When Plain Chant began to replace concert-like religious music in liturgical celebrations, Archabbot Boniface Wimmer remarked with a twinkle in his eye that he could not conceive music without "kettledrum, horns, and flutes." *page 104*

Herbert Boyer ('58) merited a portrait on the cover of *Time* magazine for his work in genetic research. *page 105*

"Hello," a painting by Roman Verostko, about 1967. *page 107*

Warner Johnson, Jr. ('93) with his aunt, Lynda Lovett. *page 110*

View toward the athletic field from Wimmer Hall. *page 119*

Apostolates of Saint Vincent Archabbey

(1790)   1846   Saint Vincent Parish, Latrobe, Pennsylvania

1846   Saint Vincent College, Latrobe, Pennsylvania

1846   Saint Vincent Seminary, Latrobe, Pennsylvania

1964   Saint Benedict Priory, Vinhedo, Brazil

1964   Wimmer Priory, Taipei, Taiwan

1967   Benedictine Priory, Savannah, Georgia

1848   Saint Benedict Parish, Carrolltown, Pennsylvania

1850   Saint Mary Parish, St. Marys, Pennsylvania

1852   Saint Joseph Parish, Johnstown, Pennsylvania

1853   Saint Lawrence Parish, Saint Lawrence, Pennsylvania

1855   Immaculate Conception Parish, New Germany, Pennsylvania

1856   Saint Martin Parish, New Derry, Pennsylvania

1859   Saint Mary Parish, Erie, Pennsylvania

1861   Saint Nicholas Parish, Nicktown, Pennsylvania

1865   Saint Boniface Parish, Chestnut Ridge, Pennsylvania

1868   Sacred Heart Parish, St. Marys, Pennsylvania

1875   Sacred Heart Parish, Youngstown, Pennsylvania

1887   Saint Bartholomew Parish, Crabtree, Pennsylvania

1889   Sacred Heart Parish, Jeannette, Pennsylvania

1890   Saint Bernard Parish, Hastings, Pennsylvania

1891   Saint Cecilia Parish, Whitney, Pennsylvania

1892   Our Lady of Perpetual Help Parish, Patton, Pennsylvania

1893   Saint Benedict Parish, Baltimore, Maryland

1896   Saint Gertrude Parish, Vandergrift, Pennsylvania

1903   Saint John Parish, Summerhill, Pennsylvania

1906   Saint Benedict Parish, Marguerite, Pennsylvania

1907   Saint George Parish, Patton, Pennsylvania

1909   Saint Mary Parish, Forbes Road, Pennsylvania

1913   Saint Bede Parish, Bovard, Pennsylvania

1918   Forty Martyrs Parish, Trauger, Pennsylvania

1919   Saint Bruno Parish, South Greensburg, Pennsylvania

1951   Queen of the World Parish, St. Marys, Pennsylvania

1957   Saint Gregory the Great Parish, Virginia Beach, Virginia

1962   Penn State Catholic Center, State College, Pennsylvania

1993   Saint Peter Parish, Pittsburgh, Pennsylvania

Wulfstan F. Clough, O.S.B.

Chronology

A.D. 529   Saint Benedict of Nursia, Italy, founds the abbey of Monte Cassino

766   Saint Michael Abbey, Metten, Bavaria, is founded

1790   Saint Vincent Parish is established on the "Sportsman's Hall Tract"

1835   Bishop Francis Patrick Kenrick of Baltimore dedicates the Parish Church under the patronage of Saint Vincent de Paul

1846   Boniface Wimmer, O.S.B., a monk of Saint Michael Abbey, Metten, Bavaria, and his companions arrive at Saint Vincent

1855   Pope Pius IX issues a decree elevating Saint Vincent monastery to the dignity of an abbey and establishes the American-Cassinese Congregation under the patronage of the Holy Guardian Angels

Pope Pius IX appoints Boniface Wimmer, O.S.B., abbot for three years

Saint Vincent Seminary is officially established through an Apostolic Brief of Pope Pius IX

1858   Saint Vincent monastic chapter elects Boniface Wimmer, O.S.B., abbot

1870   Saint Vincent (College, Seminary, and Preparatory School) is incorporated by the Legislature of the Commonwealth of Pennsylvania, which empowers it "to grant and confer degrees in the arts and sciences as are granted in other colleges and universities in the United States..."

1887   Boniface Wimmer, O.S.B., dies on December 8

1888   Andrew Hintenach, O.S.B., is elected second abbot

1892   Saint Vincent Abbey is raised to the dignity of an archabbey

Leander Schnerr, O.S.B., is elected third archabbot

Chronology (Continued)

1905   Consecration of the Archabbey Church by Bishop J. F. Regis Canevin of Pittsburgh

1913   First Lay Retreat

1918   Aurelius Stehle, O.S.B., is elected fourth archabbot

1927   Opening of the Catholic University of Peking, China, under the sponsorship of Saint Vincent Archabbey

1930   Alfred J. Koch, O.S.B., is elected fifth archabbot

1931   Benedictine Sisters from Saint Walburga Abbey, Eichstätt, Bavaria, led by Mother Leonarda Fritz, O.S.B., arrive at Saint Vincent.

1933   Saint Vincent Archabbey transfers sponsorship of the Catholic University of Peking to the Society of the Divine Word

1946   Saint Vincent observes its centennial with a Pontifical Mass, an Academic Convocation, and dedication of the renovated Crypt of the Archabbey Church

1949   Denis O. Strittmatter, O.S.B., is elected sixth archabbot

1950   Saint Vincent College football team wins the Tangerine Bowl in Orlando, Florida, by defeating Emory and Henry College of Virginia, 7-6

1963   Saint Benedict Priory, Brazil, becomes a canonical dependency of Saint Vincent Archabbey

           Rembert G. Weakland, O.S.B., is elected seventh archabbot

           Master plan for a building program is initiated after a major fire

           Wimmer Priory, Taiwan, is founded as a cononical dependency of Saint Vincent Archabbey

1967	Benedictine Priory, Savannah, Georgia, becomes a cononical dependency of Saint Vincent Archabbey
	Rembert G. Weakland, O.S.B., is elected Abbot Primate of the world-wide Benedictine Order
	Egbert H. Donovan, O.S.B., is elected eighth archabbot
1971	The Preparatory School is closed
1979	Leopold J. Krul, O.S.B., is elected ninth archabbot
1981	First lay members of the College and Seminary Board of Directors are elected
1983	Paul R. Maher, O.S.B., is elected tenth archabbot
	Saint Vincent College becomes coeducational
1987	After 56 years of service at Saint Vincent, Benedictine Sisters move to Saint Emma Monastery, Greensburg, Pennsylvania
1990	Saint Vincent Parish observes its bicentennial
1991	Douglas R. Nowicki, O.S.B., is elected eleventh archabbot
1994	Saint Vincent College women's basketball team wins the Keystone Empire Collegiate Conference championship title for the eighth time in the past ten years
1996	Saint Vincent observes its sesquicentennial

Nathan M. Cochran, O.S.B.
Omer U. Kline, O.S.B.

Contributors

THOMAS ACKLIN, O.S.B., is Rector and Associate Professor of Theology at Saint Vincent Seminary.

KURT J. BELSOLE, O.S.B., is Associate Professor of Theology and Latin at Saint Vincent Seminary.

ANTHONY G. BOSCO is Bishop of Greensburg.

WULFSTAN F. CLOUGH, O.S.B., is Lecturer in English at Saint Vincent College.

NATHAN M. COCHRAN, O.S.B., is Registrar at Saint Vincent College and Curator of the Archabbey Art Collections.

DEMETRIUS R. DUMM, O.S.B., is Professor of New Testament at Saint Vincent Seminary.

JASON Z. EDELSTEIN is Lecturer in Religious Studies at Saint Vincent College and serves as Rabbi of Temple David, Monroeville, Pennsylvania.

CAMPION P. GAVALER, O.S.B., is Associate Professor of Religious Studies at Saint Vincent College.

MARK GRUBER, O.S.B., is Assistant Professor of Sociology-Anthropology at Saint Vincent College.

TASSO KATSELAS has been architect and planner at Saint Vincent since 1964. His architectural firm is located in Pittsburgh, Pennsylvania.

ALICE KAYLOR is Associate Academic Dean and Director of the Liberal Arts Program at Saint Vincent College.

OMER U. KLINE, O.S.B., is Archivist of Saint Vincent Archabbey and Professor Emeritus of Homiletics at Saint Vincent Seminary.

DIANA B. KREILING is Manager of Community Relations and Development at Latrobe Area Hospital.

PAUL R. MAHER, O.S.B., is a retired Archabbot of Saint Vincent (1983-1990) and served as Prior at Wimmer Priory in Taiwan from 1966 to 1983.

PATRICIA McCANN, R.S.M., is Vice-President of the Institute of the Sisters of Mercy of the Americas. She taught at Saint Vincent Seminary from 1970 to 1990 and at Saint Vincent College from 1972 to 1982.

DOUGLAS R. NOWICKI, O.S.B., is Archabbot of Saint Vincent and Chancellor of Saint Vincent College and Saint Vincent Seminary.

JAMES RAGAN ('66) is Director of the Professional Writing Program at the University of Southern California.

DONALD S. RAILA, O.S.B., is Director of Oblates and Coordinator of Health Care Cost at Saint Vincent Archabbey.

FRED M. ROGERS is creator and host of *Mister Rogers' Neighborhood*, America's longest-running children's television program.

LEO ROTHRAUFF, O.S.B., is a thirty-year member of Saint Benedict Priory, Vinhedo, Brazil, and served as Prior from 1964 to 1975.

BRICE RYAN, O.S.B., is Associate Professor of Languages at Saint Vincent College and Associate Professor of Canon Law at Saint Vincent Seminary.

RICHARD SCHULTE is an alumnus of the Saint Vincent Preparatory School ('64) and College ('68).

RONALD E. TRANQUILLA is Professor of English and Chair of the English Department at Saint Vincent College.

REMBERT G. WEAKLAND, O.S.B., is Archbishop of Milwaukee. He was Archabbot of Saint Vincent from 1963 to 1967.

DONALD W. WUERL is Bishop of Pittsburgh.

For information about ordering this book, write to
The Archabbey Press
Saint Vincent Archabbey
Latrobe, Pennsylvania 15650

ISBN 1-886565-03-1

610